WILL THE DOLLARS STRETCH?

Teen Parents Living on Their Own

Virtual Reality Through Stories and Check-Writing Practice

By Sudie Pollock, M.A.

Morning Glory Press

Buena Park, California

Will the Dollars Stretch? is a good supplement for math, consumer economics,
relationship building, parenting classes, and independent study.
It provides a practical and realistic supplement to such texts as:
Teenage Couples — Coping with Reality
Teens Parenting — Your Baby's First Year
Teens Parenting — The Challenge of Toddlers
Teen Dads: Rights, Responsibilities and Joys
Surviving Teen Pregnancy
Moving On: Finding Information You Need for Living on Your Own

Library of Congress Cataloging-in-Publication Data
Pollock, Sudie, 1947-
    Will the dollars stretch? : teen parents living on their own : virtual reality
through stories and check-writing practice / by Sudie Pollock.--Rev.
        p.   cm.
    Includes bibliographical references.
    Summary: Five stories of teen parents accompanied by exercises providing
practice for the reader in writing checks and in meeting the real challenges of
living within a tight budget.
    ISBN 1-885356-78-1
    1. Home economics--Accounting--Problems, exercises, etc.--Juvenile
literature. 2. Teenage parents--Life skills guides--Juvenile literature. 3.
Checking accounts--Problems, exercises, etc.--Juvenile literature. [1. Teenage
parents. 2. Life skills. 3. Budgets, personal--Problems, exercises, etc. 4.
Checking accounts--Problems, exercises, etc.] I. Title.

TX326.P645   2001
640' .42--dc21   2001030295

MORNING GLORY PRESS, INC.
6595 San Haroldo Way   Buena Park, CA 90620
714/828-1998   FAX 714/828-2049
Printed and bound in the United States of America

CONTENTS

*Dedicated to my students
at Hill and Valley
from whom I've learned so much.*

ACKNOWLEDGMENTS

Usually the author writes this page, but Sudie Pollock gave me permission to thank those who helped make this book as realistic and accurate as possible.

First of all, I thank Sudie. This book is a model of academic integration, of combining real-life situations with math exercises, and showing young parents loving and caring for their children even as they face the challenges of independent living.

Several people read the manuscript and made valuable suggestions. Teachers included Pat Alviso and Roni Love, ABC USD Teen Parent Program, Cerritos, CA; David Crawford (our talented photographer) and Eileen Boyce, William Daylor High School, Sacramento, CA; Sharon Enright, GRADS coordinator, Ohio Department of Education. Tammy Lindsay, Lindsay Design, Boulder, CO, and Alice Jacobson, quilter extraordinaire, critiqued chapter 5. Carole Blum, Karen Blake, and Pati Lindsay proofed and proofed again. Tim Rinker designed the cover.

Jeanne Warren Lindsay, Editor

Whether you are a teenage parent, or you don't expect to have a child for years, if ever, you will probably find these stories of young parents an interesting way to learn how to write checks, keep a checking account balance, and reconcile your balance with the bank's statement each month. The stories will be most interesting if you allow yourself to "be" that person as you read.

Use Your Imagination

Try to imagine, in the first story, what it must be like to have a baby, and to depend only on welfare and food stamps for all of your financial needs. How can a single mother parent well when her income is extremely low? You will find some ideas on good parenting as well as money management in the stories.

In the second story, get into the lives of the young couple who finally have moved into their own apartment. They face the challenge of paying for everything they need with the young man's weekly paycheck. What difficulties do you think might develop in a relationship because of lack of money? How can they (you) avoid blaming each other when the money runs short? What can they (you) do to have fun that doesn't cost money? Where can they (you) economize?

For the third story, imagine you're a young mother. You have a job but you don't earn enough to pay for an apartment by yourself. You and your friend, who also has a child, decide to rent an apartment together. How can you two cooperate to make your living arrangement work?

As you read the next story, imagine you are the young man who must come to terms with his girlfriend's pregnancy. You have a part-time job and you attend school full-time. You discover that no longer can you spend your entire paycheck on your car because your coming baby must take priority in your budget. When your girlfriend moves in with you and your mother, your life becomes even more complicated.

In the fifth story, you are a young entrepreneur. You have decided to start a business of making crib quilts. You face the realities of obtaining and maintaining equipment, buying materials, working very hard at creating your product, and then, perhaps most difficult of all, marketing that product.

Perhaps you can't imagine yourself making quilts, but you think having your own business sounds inviting. Then research other possibilities for a teen to go into business. What about gardening? Car detailing? Cake decorating? Child care? Catering? It's up to you.

The best approach is to read the story through before you start working on the check-writing assignments. Take the time to think seriously about the life of this young person, and about the financial challenges you would be facing if you were in a similar situation.

Defining the Terms

Some of these checking account terms may be new to you. Before you start working on the exercises in the stories, you need a clear understanding of the following:

Balance: Amount of money in your bank account.

Check: Written order to bank to pay an amount from funds on deposit in account.

Check register: Written record of checks written and deposits made.

Deposit: Money put in a bank for safekeeping.

Outstanding: Check you have written which has not yet cleared (gone through) the bank.

Reconcile: Process of comparing your check register balance with the bank's record.

Statement: Bank's summary of transactions made in your account during statement period.

Transaction: Process of deducting or adding money to your bank account.

Keeping Track of Your Money

Your next step is to get plenty of blank checks, either from your teacher or from a bank, and start writing those day-to-day checks. Do *not* use checks from your parent's checking account, and of course the checks you use must have "Void" written on them. Check-forging is a serious crime, and that's not what you're doing!

If you prefer, you can make copies of the blank check on page 105 in the Appendix and use them to complete the exercises. You can do the same thing with the deposit ticket on page 106.

Each time you write a check, record it in your check register, and figure your new checking account balance. To do this, *subtract* the amount of your check from your previous balance.

Each time you deposit money in your account, record it in your check register — and of course you *add* the amount of the deposit to your balance.

The register is the way you keep track of your bank balance. If you don't know your bank balance, you don't know whether you can afford to write a check.

If there isn't enough money to cover the check, you have a problem. Your check will bounce — the person receiving it won't get his/her money, and you'll be charged a hefty fee.

Note that numbers followed by **C** refer to check-writing exercises, while deposits are indicated by numbers followed by **D**. Number the checks you write to match the number of that exercise. Write the number of the deposit exercise in your check register, too, as you enter those deposits.

Note that check writing, deposit entries, and account reconciliation exercises are printed in italics. This alerts you to those assignments.

Occasionally you will have a question to answer that requires neither check-writing nor deposit recording. When this happens, write the exercise number in your check register *as if* it were a check. Write your answer in the "Transactions" section on the register, and *circle your answer.* This will help you remember that number is *not* part of your bank balance record.

Using Your Check Register

For these assignments, use the following format for your check register:

Date	Check No.	Transaction	Amount of check	Deposit Amount	Balance
3/28	1D	Deposit		$505.00	$505.00
3/29	2C	Mrs. Lena	375.00		375.00
		Balance			130.00
3/31	3C	PG&E	75.00		75.00
		Balance			55.00
4/1	4C	Payless	13.84		13.84
		Balance			41.16
4/2	5C	Long's	12.23		12.23
		Balance			28.93
4/3	6FS	Food stamps: $280-54.88=$225.12			

*Keeping a careful record of all
checking account transactions is extremely important.*

Check registers are available in various styles. Some checkbooks provide a carbon copy of each check you write, but you still need to keep track of those checks in your check register. For these assignments, you can make copies of the check register form on page 107.

Check your math very carefully. If you make one mistake, that mistake will mean your balance will be wrong in the assignments that follow. Use a pencil as you fill in your check register so you can erase any mistakes you make.

When you need to add items and/or figure the sales tax (as required for **5C** and **7C,** for example, on page 19), do your math on another sheet of paper. Number your work to match the check exercise, and turn that paper in to your teacher along with your completed checks and check register.

Writing Readable Checks

If you're not sure how to write checks properly, study the following example carefully before you start. A check *must* be written legibly *in ink*. It's okay to print everything except your signature — some of us find printing is easier for other people to read than is our writing.

Whether you print or use cursive writing, take your time. When you write checks in real life, you want them to be read accurately.

Ask your teacher to check your work after you've completed ten of the check-writing and bank deposit assignments. S/he can advise you on the best way to complete the rest of your assignments.

At the end of each month in each story, you will be checking on your math yourself by reconciling your checking account balance with the statement given in the story. See directions on page 108.

Your Final Assignment

Write a paper in which you react to the lives of the young people in these stories. If you were a single mother living on welfare, how do you think you would feel? Would you believe you had choices? What might you do to work toward the life you want?

If you were the young woman in the second story, how might you react to the money problems this young couple is facing? How could you parent your child well, yet help your partner with the financial support of your family? If you were the young man, how could you make more money, now or later? Would you expect your partner to work full-time? If so, what would you do about childcare?

As you read the next story, think about problems that might occur when two young mothers and their children live together. Offer suggestions for making life easier for all of them.

The teen father in the fourth story is overwhelmed by his partner's pregnancy. His part-time job barely covers the basic expenses of pregnancy. How will he support a child? He considers dropping out of school, then decides his baby deserves more than a dropout father. What would *you* do? Why?

After you read the fifth story, write an essay in which you discuss teen entrepreneurship (developing your own business rather than working for someone else). Include two or three possibilities for developing a business. Also discuss the pitfalls of such a plan.

Remember — read the story first. Then go back and read it again and complete the exercises. Complete these assignments by writing your reactions to the lives of these young people.

Your child is very important to you.

CHAPTER 1

You Are a Single Parent

Last June, you graduated from a special high school program for teen mothers. With your diploma in hand, you think you have it made, but you don't have a job, your baby is now a toddler, and on top of it all, your mom is being evicted because the owner wants to move into the house. Even though she hasn't said it, you can tell that it would be easier for her to find the housing she wants and can afford if you and your child weren't part of the picture.

Wow! You had counted on living with your mom for awhile — hoping your ex-boyfriend would get his life together eventually so he could get an apartment and ask you to join him. Oh well, another dream down the tubes! You've heard girls at school talking about being on

Welfare, or Aid, but when you were underage, you didn't
qualify because your mom wasn't on Welfare herself.

Now that you've had your 18th birthday, you decide to
look into it. You take your child on the bus and go to the
Social Services Department across town. You talk to a
receptionist and read a pamphlet. You find out that as a
single mother, you may qualify for TANF, Temporary
Assistance for Needy Families. The amount is $505 a
month. This used to be called Welfare or AFDC (Aid to
Families with Dependent Children) and is money from
taxpayers. There are new rules now.

You are allowed to receive assistance for only two years
at a time, and only for five years in your entire life, no
matter how many children you have. You are expected to
enroll in a trade school or college program — you can't
just stay home, because if you did, that's exactly where
you'd be in two years when your grant runs out. You plan
to take a class or two at the local community college to get
ready for a job — and a career — besides the career of
being a parent.

Another part of the new TANF rules is that you have a
caseworker, a person who meets with you every month to
make sure you're going to school and getting on with
your life.

Along with TANF, you can also apply for Food Stamps
which will give you coupons worth $280 to spend on food
each month for yourself and your child. You can't buy
steak, but if you are careful and watch the grocery store
sales, you might be able to feed yourself and your child for
a month. You can also apply for Medi-Cal, a medical
insurance program funded by state taxpayers. The problem
is that not all doctors will accept a person who is on this
program since there is a lot of paperwork involved and
sometimes the State is slow in paying the doctor for

care provided.

All this help sounds really good, but you discover that you also have to cooperate with the District Attorney's office and file a Paternity Action which names your ex-boyfriend as the father of your child. Since your boyfriend is 18, he will pay child support based on his earning potential. Those payments last for 18 years and are part of the money you get from TANF. After all, you and he are really responsible for your child's support, not the state taxpayers.

Even though your mom isn't crazy about you going on Aid, you decide to apply. You already know, from reading the pamphlet, that you need to make an appointment and bring in your child's birth certificate and your own, both of your social security cards plus proof that you live in this county. Usually something addressed to you will prove that you live here.

It takes a while to get your own birth certificate since you were born in another area. Your boyfriend is out of town so you have to ask your mom for money to pay for a copy of your child's birth certificate — it's $8.00. You wonder if you will ever really be independent!

After three weeks, you get a check in the mail. It is for $505. You decide to get a checking account so you can keep track of how you spend your money. You know that because you were a student in the district, you can use the services of the Napa Schools Credit Union. You open an account and get a packet of checks. You realize that if you couldn't use the credit union, you'd have monthly bank charges you'd need to deduct from your account balance. You're glad you don't have *that* expense.

Deposit the TANF money in your checking account. **(1D)** See the check register example on page 11 and the deposit ticket on page 106.

You vow to keep an exact record of the money in your

checking account. Every time you write a check, you'll *subtract* the amount from your balance. Every time you deposit your check, you'll *add* it to your balance.

Finding an Apartment

You start looking in the paper for a place to rent since you really want to have a place of your own. You find several, and you get a friend to drive you around to look at them. The first one is a dump. The second one is in a bad neighborhood. The third one has no yard for your child.

The fourth one is on the third floor of a building that only has stairs. The last one is very small, needs to be cleaned, but has a small yard that is fenced. It seems like a safe place so you decide to take it.

The ad in the paper said the rent was $325 with a deposit of $300. You only have $505 for the entire month. So you talk to the owner, and she agrees to let you pay one month's rent now plus $50 of the deposit fee each month for six months.

Write your first check to Mrs. Lena for the rent plus the deposit. (**2C**) See the example on page 12, and the check form on page 105.

How much do you have left? This is your checking account balance as shown in your check register. (See example on page 11.) This helps you keep track of every check you write, and you will be able to see where your money is going.

Costs of Moving In

Now that you have a place, you need to get the utilities hooked up: the gas stove, the lights, the heater. That means you need to call PG&E (the gas and electric company) and have the service turned on. They require a deposit of $75. *Write the check for the deposit.* (**3C**)

You also want to have a phone, so you call Pacific Bell. You discover there is a charge of $45 to hook up the phone. You decide to wait until next month for a phone.

Your new place needs to be cleaned so you have to buy a broom, mop, cleanser, Lysol, and a bucket. The total comes to $13.84. *Write a check to Payless for these items.* (**4C**)

Your girlfriend offers to help you clean. Together, you scrub the kitchen sink and counters, scrub the toilet, sink, and shower, mop the floors, wipe walls and windows. You also clean the refrigerator and the oven. The place finally looks like something you want to live in.

Now you need several other items:

Paper towels	.69	Kleenex	2.03
Toilet paper	1.09	Shampoo	2.59
Light bulbs	1.29	Toothpaste	.89
Ant traps	2.79		

Figure the subtotal, then add 7.5 percent sales tax. *Write a check to Long's for the total.* (**5C**)

You go to Safeway and buy food for yourself and your child. The bill comes to $54.88, which you pay with food stamps. What are your remaining stamps worth? (**6FS**) *List your answer as shown in the example on page 11.*

Now you have food in your kitchen. You're feeling pretty good about your little place.

A week later, your child falls down and scrapes his knee. You realize you have no first aid supplies so you walk to Long's. *Write a check for these items at the listed prices plus tax of 7.5 percent.* (**7C**)

Band Aids	2.99
First aid cream	3.25
Hydrogen peroxide	.89

On the weekend, a friend comes by, and you go shopping. You find a cute shirt for your child. *Write a check to Mervyn's for $10.73.* **(8C)**

After Mervyn's you walk down to the Goodwill second-hand store on Main Street and you find three shirts for $2 each including tax. *Write a check.* **(9C)**

You make a mental note to stay out of Mervyn's and always check out the second-hand clothing stores before you buy anything. You and your friends used to talk about how you'd never buy clothes in a second-hand store, but you're finding it's not a bad way to go after all.

Your friend wants to go to the show, but you think spending $7.50 on a movie isn't such a good idea. You talk her into watching the kids at the skateboard park instead. Your child loves watching them, but you can tell that your friend is bored.

Your friend has to get ready for a date tonight so she drops you off. You spend 15 minutes playing puppets with your child, read to your child for half an hour, then you go outside together and listen to the birds. After you make tuna sandwiches, beans, and oranges for dinner, you bathe your child, read another story, and get ready for bed.

Another friend who has a new baby calls and asks you to baby-sit tomorrow from 9 p.m. until 9 the next morning. You think she's crazy to leave her child for so long, but she is willing to pay you $20 for the time. When she arrives with the baby, the child is wet and crying.

You change him, feed him, burp him, and rock him to sleep. You ask your child to help put the baby to sleep by singing to him, and you both sing for about an hour. You are glad to see the little guy go home in the morning, and you think about how hard it would be if you had two children to care for. *Be sure to deposit the $20 in your account.* **(10D)**

Off to the Laundromat

Your laundry is piling up and you need to get it done. Since nobody is available to take you to the laundromat, you get out your child's red wagon and load up your dirty clothes. Your child sits in the wagon with the clothes and thinks this is lots of fun.

On your way to the laundromat, you stop at the credit union. *Write a check to Cash for $10 because you need quarters for the machines.* (**11C**)

Your period starts at the laundromat, and you go to the nearby store to get tampons. While you're there, you decide to get a box of crackers and some cheese for lunch. You left your food stamps at home. *Write a check to Vallerga's for $10.95.* (**12C**) You make a promise that you will pack a lunch from now on when you go out.

Later that week, you run out of groceries so you buy $74.43 worth at Safeway, using your food stamps. You are careful to buy only enough fresh fruit for a few days so it doesn't spoil. You buy the house brands which are a bit cheaper so your stamps last longer. *Figure the amount of stamps you have left for this month.* (**13FS**)

It is now the end of the month. You look at your check register and see that you have only $3.58 left. If you run out of milk, you can get more using food stamps, but if you are low on toilet paper, there is little money left.

One night your child starts running a fever and coughing. You get really scared and decide that you have to get a phone. They will bill you next month for the installation.

Reconciling Your Bank Statement

Your bank statement arrives today. You look at it, and at first, you think there must be some mistake. According to your records, you have exactly $3.58 left in your checking account, but the bank says you have $31.26. Maybe you have more money than you thought. Wouldn't that be great?

This statement covers Month One.			
Summary	**Checks/Withdrawals**		**Deposits**
Previous balance 00.00	2C 375.00	7C 7.67	1D 505.00
Deposits 525.00	3C 75.00	11C 10.00	10D 20.00
Withdrawals 493.74	4C 13.84		
New Balance **31.26**	5C 12.23		

So you decide to figure it out. You find the form on the back of the bank statement that tells you how to "reconcile" the bank's numbers with yours. (See page 108. Make a copy of the form.)

First, you see if all your checks have been sent from the stores to the bank. If the bank hasn't gotten the check you wrote, you realize that amount has *not* been deducted from your account. These are your "outstanding" checks.

Sure enough, there are three checks missing from the statement. So you subtract the total of those checks from the bank's ending balance. Now it matches your balance.

You haven't made a mistake after all. Now you know why your math teacher used to insist you do all those adding and subtracting exercises. And you thought you'd never use your math!

Month Two — Your Check Is Late

Your check doesn't arrive on the first of the month. You call your case worker and she says it's in the mail. By the fourth of the month, the check still isn't there.

You call again. She is ill and nobody else knows about your check. Your landlady wants her rent and her deposit money. Finally, on the fifth, your check arrives. *Deposit it in your account* (**14D**) *and enter it on your register.*

Your landlady charges you $5 extra for being late. *Write a check to Mrs. Lena for the rent plus $50 for the partial deposit due this month plus the late charge.* **(15C)**

The $45 bill for the phone installation comes. *Write a check to Pacific Bell for $45.* **(16C)**

You have no stamps to mail your letters. *Write a check to the Postmaster for a book of stamps: $6.80.* **(17C)**

The gas and electric bill arrives. You call PG&E and learn you're on a special rate for low income families. *Write a check to PG&E for $20.38.* **(18C)**

Your phone bill for last month arrives. You qualify for a low income rate and started your service late in the month. Your bill is only $8.60. *Write a check to Pacific Bell.* **(19C)**

The Expenses Continue

You would like to enroll your child in some play activities through the Recreation Department. There are gymnastics classes where the parent goes with the child. They cost $5. *Write a check.* **(20C)**

A friend told you about bus passes for people who ride regularly. You decide to buy one since the cost is $15 for 20 rides. Your child loves to ride the bus and see everything. *Write a check to Napa Transit.* **(21C)** Plan to buy a pass every month.

Your friend with the baby boy calls to ask you to babysit again. She has to go to the hospital overnight to have a biopsy done on her cervix. She says that she may have cervical cancer and is really scared. The doctor thinks it may be from her having had several sex partners already in her short life. You think that her life might become even shorter if she has cancer. She is only seventeen.

You didn't sleep much because her baby has a cold and was awake several times during the night. Thankfully your child slept through it. When your friend comes to pick up her son, she hands you a twenty dollar bill. You hug her and wish her luck. *Be sure to deposit the twenty dollars into your account.* (**22D**)

You are running low on household supplies. Take the bus to Payless where there is a sale. You buy:

3 pkg. toilet paper @ .79 *each*		Deodorant	2.49
3 bars soap for showers	1.99	Nail polish	1.99
2 rolls of paper towels	1.00	Hand lotion	1.89
Baby shampoo	1.99	Baby vitamins	3.76
Advil for cramps	3.59	Hair spray	1.99
3 cans of cleanser	1.00	Soap for dishes	1.89
Tampax	2.25	Laundry soap	5.99

Total all of these items, add 7.5 percent sales tax. *Write a check to Payless for the total.* (**23C**)

Wow! That took a chunk out of your money! It's still early in the month and you have paid all your bills, but you have only $11.04 left.

Some Things Are Free

A friend wants you to go to the water slides next weekend. Can you get someone to watch your child? Can you spend the money you have left for that? You decide to pass.

You take your child to the library and check out some books for free. Your child is delighted and asks to go back to the "liberry" every day. You make it a point to go at least once a week on Wednesday for the Children's Story Hour at 10 A.M.

Even though you have decided not to have sex until you're married, an old boyfriend has been stopping by to see you. You still like him and you worry that you might get pregnant again if you do have sex. You and your child take the bus to the Health Department and pick up some free condoms when you get your WIC coupons. You realize that these free items are really paid for by California tax-payers. You tell yourself that you're going to get off public assistance as soon as you can get a good job.

In the meantime, you're glad you get help from WIC (Women, Infant and Children Food Program). The coupons are for milk and other nutritious foods for your child.

Help from Grandma

Your grandmother sends you a check for $100 just because she loves you. You really want to spend it on something fun — have your nails done or get a perm, but you know better. You are living an adult life now and you have to make adult decisions. That means doing the right thing for your family.

You deposit the entire check into your account **(24D)** and call your grandmother to tell her how much her thoughtful-ness meant to you. You also bake her some cookies, take the bus to her house, and give her a big kiss along with the cookies. She hugs you and tells you that she's proud of the great job you're doing with your child.

You haven't had any curtains in your apartment because you couldn't afford them. You decide to use part of your grandmother's gift for curtains. You go to K-Mart and find some blue and white checkered curtains for your kitchen and a light green pair for your bedroom. *Write a check to K-Mart for $46.73.* **(25C)**

Looking Good for Your Job Interview

Your caseworker calls and suggests you set up a job interview with the manager at Carole's Family Cafe. You need to wear a black skirt, a white shirt, and black shoes. You and your child take the bus to Goodwill and buy both a skirt and shirt for $5, tax included. What a deal! *Write a check.* **(26C)**

Next, you and your child go to K-Mart for shoes. *Write a check for $12.53.* **(27C)** Your child has a crying fit in K-Mart but you handle it well by simply picking up your screaming child and your package, and calmly walking to the bus stop.

Your friend told you last week she'd watch your child for a few hours so you could get out. You figure this is the time to take her up on her offer. She agrees to watch your child while you go to the job interview, looking good. Several other people are also interviewing for the job. You see some girls who went to school with you. You all ask about each other's children. You hear about one girl who had her child taken away because her boyfriend used drugs around the child. You vow never to let that happen to your child.

That night you fix spaghetti for dinner, much to your child's delight. You add carrots and apples to the menu because you want your child to get plenty of vitamins and minerals.

After cleaning up, baths, and storytime, you put your child to bed.

After a week, you are notified that you didn't get the job. You feel bad and think that if you just had the *Napa Valley Register* delivered to your door every day, you could find out about and apply for jobs more easily — or if you had a computer, you could check the internet. Then you remember that the library has the newspaper and computers for free. You decide to save your money and go to the library more often.

Costs of Parenting

Your child wants to go back to the gymnastics class, but you don't think you can afford it this month. You take your child to the park instead and teach him about the slide, the swings, and the water fountain.

Your old stroller broke and you can't fix it. You really need one because your child is very heavy to carry around when he's asleep. You go to the second-hand shops and find a stroller for $20. *Write a check to Blum's Recyclables for $20.* (**28C**)

While you are in the shop, you see a little pedal car that your child really likes. You ask if you can put it on lay-away. The clerk says yes . . . if you put $10 down on it now. The rest of the money, $12, will be due next month. *Write another check to Blum's Recylables for the down payment.* (**29C**)

Your ex-boyfriend's parents have always supplied the disposable diapers you needed. They just called to say they can't afford to do that anymore. They offered to get you started with a diaper service, and you will have to pay $55 each month.

What About Next Month?

You start getting worried about all these bills you have to pay "next month." Will you have enough money? You write down what you owe:

Tidee Didee Diaper Service	$55.00
Pedal car — last payment	12.00

How will you afford these bills on top of the other ones?

You think: I'll write down a budget and *stick to it.* That means *no extra expenses!*

Rent	$325	Diapers	55
Deposit	50	Pedal car	12
Phone	12	Bus pass	15
PG&E	20	Laundry	20

Figure the total. **(30)** *Will your check cover all these expenses?* **(31)** And don't forget, you will have other expenses not covered by food stamps such as toothpaste and other non-food items.

Another bank statement arrived today. You know what to do with it this time. When you've finished your figuring, does the bank's balance match yours?

This statement covers Month Two.						
Summary	**Checks/Withdrawals**				**Deposits**	
Previous balance 31.26	8C	10.73	18C	20.38	14D	505.00
Deposits 625.00	9C	6.00	19C	8.60	22D	20.00
Withdrawals 591.95	12C	10.95	20C	5.00	24D	100.00
New Balance $64.31	15C	380.00	21C	15.00		
	16C	45.00	23C	36.76		
	17C	6.80	25C	46.73		

Another Late Check

Your check is late again. It finally arrives on the fifth and *you deposit it.* **(32D)** Mrs. Lena is getting upset. She says she never should have rented to someone on welfare. You feel terrible and offer to pay her another $5 late charge. She agrees. *Write her a check for the rent, the late charge, and this month's $50 toward the deposit.* **(33C)**

You think to yourself: three more months and I'll have that deposit paid off. That will mean an extra $50 every month. At least she let you pay it off this way. You could never have afforded this place if she hadn't.

All Those Bills Again

With your check in the credit union, you set out to pay your bills. You and your child take the bus to Blum's Recyclables and pay for the pedal car. *Write a check for $12.* **(34C)** Your PG&E bill is $21.45, your phone bill to Pacific Bell is $12.50, and you need to buy another bus pass for

$15. *Write checks to the appropriate places.* (**35C, 36C, 37C**) *Also write a $55.00 check to Tidee Didee Diaper Service.* (**38C**)

Every time you go to the store for food, you are grateful for food stamps. Some of the clerks make you feel dumb, but most of them are nice about it. They have to count the stamps out and make sure what you bought is legally paid for by food stamps. You know you can't buy non-food items with your stamps.

You run into a friend in the park. She also has a child. She says she is paying about $80 a month for disposable diapers. You're glad you have diaper service. You two talk about how hard it is to save any money, how you never get to buy any new clothes for yourself, and how tired you are of never having enough money.

She says she heard that young mothers only get two years on welfare, and then they have to get a job. You talk about how nice it would be to have a job and earn more money than you get on welfare. Your friend has a new sweetie and wants to go to the movies tonight. You offer to watch her toddler, and she agrees to pay you $10. Deposit that amount in your checking account. (**39D**)

Another Day of Laundry

You really need to do laundry again, so you get the wagon and load it up. Walking to the laundromat, you teach your child about crossing streets, waiting for the green light, and looking both ways for cars. You see a carload of girls you used to hang out with. They wave, and you worry that they will think you are homeless — pulling around a child's wagon full of clothes.

You need quarters for the machines, so you stop at the credit union. *Write a check to Cash for $10.* (**40C**) The teller asks for ID, but you don't have a driver's license. You do have your Medi-Cal card which you show her.

When you get to the laundromat, you realize you forgot soap. Rather than go all the way home to get it, you buy some from the machine for $1, and you think: I've got to get more organized! It costs too much to not plan ahead.

After the laundry is done, you head for home. Your child is tired and so are you. You read about five books together and play with Play-Doh. Dinner tonight will be something simple. You heat up some soup, make cheese sandwiches, and peel an orange for yourself and one for your child. You'd like to stop by Burger King and get something, but spending $3.50 for food isn't in your budget.

After your child is fed, bathed, and put to bed, you do dishes and clean up the kitchen. Then you put away the clean laundry, wipe down the stroller where your child spilled grape juice, take off your old nail polish and decide not to put more on — it gets chipped too easily.

Your porch light burned out so you take a chair outside and climb up and replace the light. You notice that the back yard needs to be watered but you don't have a hose. You wonder if Mrs. Lena will give you a hose. You go back inside and *write her a letter asking her to do that.* **(41-letter)** You remember the form for a letter from when you took the business letter test in school.

Your Child Gets Sick

Your child gets sick again and you call the doctor. You take your child on the bus to the doctor. After the visit, you both take the bus to Payless to get your prescription filled. The medicine isn't covered by Medi-Cal so you have to pay for it. *Write a check for $8.69.* **(42C)**

You wander around the store and see some yarn in a beautiful new color. You think about making an afghan to put over the sofa in your apartment. You have a crochet hook somewhere, and you'd enjoy crocheting in the evening. The yarn price is $1.49, and you need six skeins. Since it sometimes goes on sale for $1, you decide to wait.

Your child is sick for several days, and you stay home heating up chicken noodle soup and reading stories to your child. You sometimes wish you had a TV and cable, but that's another expense you can't afford. Your child really loves books anyway, so you don't worry about no TV.

In fact, you brought home a book for yourself, too, last time you were at the library. You chose *Detour for Emmy* because it's the story of a teenage single mother. You find that, as you read, you recognize parts of yourself in *Emmy.*

Having a stroller has helped. You just pop your child into it and away you go. It would be great to have a car, but how in the world would you pay for gas? and insurance? and oil? and registration? It's just better to take the bus.

Will Your Life Change?

One of your friends offers to take care of your child for an evening so you can have some free time. You think about what you want to do. Go shopping, but not buy anything? Stay home and read? Go hang out with people who used to be your friends but who don't have the responsibilities you do? Go to the movies with someone? Who pays? Go visit your parents? Your sister or brother? Go for a walk? Alone? Call your ex-boyfriend? Find a new love?

Before you get too depressed, you think about your future. You can't be on welfare forever, so what would you like to do for a job? You walk to the park with a notebook and a pen. You write down all the jobs you can think of that you see around you. Bus driver . . . bank teller . . . welfare worker . . . public health nurse . . . diaper delivery person . . . PG&E . . . phone company . . . police officer . . . fire fighter . . . mail carrier . . .

Lots of people have lots of jobs. There has to be one out there for you! You decide to call the Training and Employment Center and make an appointment.

This being on welfare is not so great although you do get to spend all day with your child. But sometimes you wish you didn't have to be with your child *all* day. The idea of having a job and also spending time with your child sounds better and better.

Another friend calls and asks if you can watch her child all day because she's signed up for a full day of career testing. You say sure, you'll do it for $20, which you could really use. She says she can only pay you $10. You two discuss it and come to an agreement: She will pay you $15. *Deposit that into your checking account.* (**43D**)

Of Afghans and Mops and Bridal Showers

On the way home from the park, you drop by the library to read the *Napa Valley Register*. There is a sale on yarn at Payless! You already found your crochet hook in your jewelry box. Next day you and your child take the bus to Payless and buy six skeins. *Write a check for $6.45.* (**44C**)

On the bus ride back home, you think of the beautiful afghan you are going to make. Dinner that night is chili from a can and cornmeal muffins you make from a mix, and bananas. It tastes pretty good, and your child eats a lot.

After you get your child bathed and put to bed, you clean up the kitchen like you do every night. The kitchen floor needs to be mopped since you spilled apple juice this morning, so you get the mop and do that. Then you notice that the refrigerator smells so you clean that out and find moldy tomato sauce in the back.

You think about the things you saw in the window at Mervyn's. You'd like to buy some matching bath towels on sale, but they're $5 each. You decide to wait.

It doesn't seem fair that people who get married have showers, but people like yourself who have the same needs don't have showers. You would have lots of towels and sheets and pillowcases and blankets and probably dishes that match and silverware and even a set of glasses if you'd had a bridal shower. As it is, you have a few pieces of silverware that match and some mugs that are the same color, but most of your dishes are what your mom had left over. Maybe there is something to be said for waiting to have sex until you're married. At least you'd have new sheets.

What About Christmas Gifts?

You're thinking about what you can give people for the Christmas holidays. On TANF, you can't afford much. You'd at least like to send Christmas cards to your friends.

You and your child take the bus downtown and go to K-Mart to look at cards. You're horrified at the prices. The ones you like are $2 or $3 *each.* You can't afford them.

How about making them? You decide to buy some sheets of green cardstock and make Christmas postcards. You also buy a silver marking pen. *Write a check for $8.45.* **(45C)**

It's time to reconcile your bank statement again:

This statement covers Month Three.						
Summary		**Checks/Withdrawals**				**Deposits**
Previous balance	64.31	26C	5.00	36C	12.50	32D 505.00
Deposits	515.00	27C	12.53	37C	15.00	39D 10.00
Withdrawals	540.72	28C	20.00	38C	55.00	
New Balance	38.59	29C	10.00	40C	10.00	
		33C	380.00	42C	8.69	
		34C	12.00			

Month Four — and Your Check Is on Time

Your check arrives on the second of the month so Mrs. Lena doesn't charge you a late fee. *Deposit your check.*

(46D) *Write a check for the rent and this month's $50 deposit.* **(47C)** Mrs. Lena also brings you a hose.

Pay the Tidee Didee Diaper Service $55. **(48C)**
Pay PG&E's bill: $15.95. **(49C)**
Pay the phone bill: $12.50 to Pacific Bell. **(50C)**
Buy another bus pass: $15, Napa Transit. **(51C)**

When you go to Safeway to buy groceries, you have to take the bus and carry all your groceries with you. There must be an easier way. What about taking the wagon you use for your laundry? Your child likes to ride in it, and it would work just fine. You can't take the wagon on the bus so you have to walk with your child and the empty wagon. Along the way, you teach your child a song or two, you count the trees, and you teach the color red. Your child says, "wed," but you think that's pretty good.

At Safeway, you pull the wagon inside and load up all the things you need. You pay for the food with food stamps and WIC coupons. You wanted to buy mascara, but it isn't on sale, so you wait. You think Payless prices are better anyway.

On the way home, you run into some kids you used to know. They ask you what you're doing. You explain that since you don't have a car, the wagon is the easiest way to carry groceries. They all say your child is really cute and getting big. They don't offer to baby-sit for you or take you out for a hamburger.

Mom's Role Versus Dad's

You pass by the homeless shelter and think about what you would do if you didn't have welfare. Your ex-boyfriend is supposed to pay child support but that money, if he pays it, goes to the District Attorney who sends it to the Welfare Department, and then it's sent to you.

It seems unfair that all he has to do is pay some money

and you have to do everything else. You have the cleaning, the laundry, the bathing, the cooking, the shopping, the worrying, the planning, the day in and day out work of raising a child, and all he has to do is pay some money.

You've heard that he is hanging around with another girl, younger than you, who has a car. You wonder if he's having sex with her. You wonder if he's saying the same things to her that he said to you. Things like "I love you" and "I'll always be there" and "I'll never leave you" and "I can handle it." Right.

When you get home, you ask your child if dinner should be tomato soup and a toasted cheese sandwich or canned spaghetti and meatballs. You fix whatever your child chooses. You also fix apples for the two of you. They were on sale last time you were in the store. You'd have enjoyed peaches or pears, but you know that buying fruit in season is a lot cheaper, and apples are in season now.

Time to Visit Your Mom

Your mom calls a few days later and invites you to come over for lunch. You haven't seen much of your mom since you moved out. It was hard to live together, and she let you know you had to grow up fast if you wanted to stay pregnant and raise a child. Now you wonder what she wants.

You and your child take the bus over to her house. Your mom is delighted to see her grandchild, and says she misses you both. She has fixed a nice lunch and asks you if you need help. You don't want to ask for money because you want to be able to support yourself, but you could use her help in other ways. You say you'll think about it.

After you talk for awhile, she gives you $20, hugs you both, and thanks you for coming over. On your way home, you stop by Payless and buy mascara. *Write a check for $6.55.* (**52C**) *Deposit your $20 in your account.* (**53D**)

That night you make a meatloaf for dinner, and you let your child pour catsup over the top before you bake it. You also make baked potatoes and your child rubs each potato with vegetable oil before you put them into the oven. You and your child make lemon pudding and oatmeal cookies. You want your child to remember you as a good mom.

Helping the Money Stretch

You think about how you could make a little more money, and you remember about recycling. If you save plastic liter bottles and glass bottles and aluminum cans, you can sell them to the machines in front of Nob Hill grocery store. Great!

You make a plan to gather all the recyclables you find as you walk to the store or play in the park with your child. You'll also check the trash container area in your apartment building, and pick up the cans and bottles other people throw away. Good thinking!

It's getting colder and your child needs a pair of jeans and a sweatshirt. You find some you like at K-Mart. *Write a check for $14.71, including sales tax.* (**54C**)

You have a bad toothache and you call a dentist. You know Medi-Cal does not cover dental work, but your tooth really hurts. The dentist agrees to see you for $30. *Write a $30 check to Dr. Grinn.* (**55C**)

Month Five

You are really tired of cooking a meal every night so when a friend drops by and asks you to go for a pizza, you grab your child and go. The bill at Pizza Hut is $10.89. *You write a check.* (**56C**) Your friend gives you a $5 bill for her part. *Deposit the $5 into your account.* (**57D**)

Your bank statement arrived two days ago, and you're just now getting around to comparing the bank's numbers with yours. Is everything okay?

This statement covers Month Four.					
Summary		**Checks/Withdrawals**		**Deposits**	
Previous balance 38.59	35C 21.45	49C 15.95	43D 15.00
Deposits 540.00	44C 6.45	51C 15.00	46D 505.00
Withdrawals 533.85	45C 8.45	52C 6.55	53D 20.00
New Balance **44.74**	47C 375.00	55C 30.00	
	48C 55.00		

Your check is on time again. *You take it to the credit union and deposit it in your account.* (**58D**)

The rent is due again. *Write a rent check for $325 plus this month's $50 deposit.* (**59C**)

You wonder when your child will be ready to be potty trained, but then you think about how expensive "pull-ups" are. You don't think you can afford them. For now, the diaper service is a real money saver. Maybe your child will stay in diapers until you can afford to buy some real underwear that you can wash out at home. Kids are so expensive!

You have these bills to pay: PG&E, $15.50; Pacific Bell, $12.50; Bus pass, $15. *Write the checks.* (**60C, 61C, 62C**)

You're running out of toilet paper, paper towels, toothpaste, babywipes, cleaning supplies, and mouthwash. Actually, you don't think you can afford mouthwash! You take your child to Safeway in the wagon and buy the economy (huge) package of toilet paper and the other items. *Write a check for $68.78.* (**63C**)

Pulling the wagon back to your place, you see your ex-boyfriend driving his new girlfriend's car. He sees you pulling a wagon with 24 rolls of toilet paper in it and laughs. He doesn't even notice his child who is sitting safely in the back of the wagon.

Those $ Decisions

It is the fifth of the month, you have all your bills paid, and you have $29.86 left in your checking account. You have some serious thinking to do.

There are things you would really like to buy but you know you have to decide if they are things you just *want* or things you really *need*. The *needs* come first. So you make a list of wants and needs. First, the needs:

> *Take your child to the dentist for the first time.*
> *Get your eyes checked for glasses.*
> *Buy shoes for your child.*

Now the wants:

> *Buy yourself a pair of shoes for the summer.*
> *Get a kitten or puppy for you and your child.*
> *Get new curtains for the bedroom.*
> *Get your fingernails done.*
> *Change your hair color; keep it up for six months.*

It dawns on you that welfare doesn't give you more money during Christmas or on your child's birthday. You never really knew what people meant when they said being a teen mother meant you would be "in poverty" or poor. Now you know.

Other Ways to Live

You also know that the only way out is to get a better education, get a good job, and not have more children. You have seen your friends and what happened to their lives.

One girl married a guy and they have two kids. She has to ask her husband to give her money for food and clothes for the kids. If she wants anything for herself he says they can't afford it. Yet, he spends money on his car and buys beer for his buddies. He won't let her go back to school nor will he let her get a job. He says her job is taking care of the family.

Another friend has three children and lives with a guy

who isn't the father of any of them. You don't think that's a great way to raise kids. You think she just let him move in because he would help pay the rent. She says she wants to have his baby, but you told her to get the Depo-Provera shot every three months.

Another of your friends still lives with her mom and stepdad. They pay for some of her expenses and that helps. She is going to Napa Valley College. She lets them know where she is going and what she is doing. They let her use the car. Her life doesn't sound so bad, but yours is very different.

Another friend lives with her boyfriend and has no kids. They both work and make enough money to have a really nice place, two cars, and they go away once a month together to have what she calls "our romantic weekend." She is planning their wedding and has asked you to be a bridesmaid. You don't think you can afford the dress.

Get Going — To Your Future

You can see that there are lots of ways to live, but it depends upon how much money you have. If you are poor, your options are fewer than if you can pay your own way.

Even though you get lonely sometimes and wish you had an adult around, you really love your child, and you know you need to give yourself to that little person now. You also need to get some job training and stop thinking that some-one else is going to "save" you from your situation.

You're glad you signed up for those computer classes. You want to get off welfare as soon as you can. So rather than spend energy on a new relationship, you're going to put your energy into yourself and become the best mom and grown-up you can be.

Get going!

Supporting a family is a challenge these days.

CHAPTER 2

You and Your Partner Move Out

For this story, you are 17 and your child is eight months old. At the end of summer, you'll be starting your senior year of high school. Your boyfriend, who is the father of your baby, is 18 and has been working full-time since he passed the GED (General Education Development) exam.

Now that you've had your child, you and your boyfriend want to get a place together. You know you can't collect TANF (welfare) if you live with the father of your baby, but since he has a job, you two think you can manage.

Figuring Your Net Pay

First, you need to know how much money he makes every week. His job pays $7.75 per hour and he works 40 hours per week. *Multiply the hourly wage by 40.* (**1**) This amount is his weekly *gross pay.*

That seems like something you could live on, right?
Maybe. The next thing you have to do is subtract taxes.
First, figure out 13 percent (.13) of the total for taxes. *Sub-tract that from the gross.* (**2**) That final figure is *take home pay* or *net pay.* This is what you have for living expenses.

Check with your teacher to make sure your math is right. If your amount is wrong here, all the rest of your checkbook figuring will be wrong.

Where Will You Live?

The first thing you want to do is find a place to live.
Look in the paper for two-bedroom apartments, duplexes,
and houses. You call several places and look around for two
weeks. Some places are too small, some have no stove or
refrigerator (and you don't have either a stove or a refrigerator). Some don't have a play area for your child, and
some are in places you wouldn't want to live. You finally
settle on a two-bedroom duplex in the downtown area.

The rent is $695 per month with a $600 deposit.

Your boyfriend has been saving up, so he has the full
amount. In fact, he has $1,585.84 in his checking account.
You volunteer to be the family accountant. On a Thursday,
you write a check to your new landlady, Ms. Amador, for
one month's rent plus the deposit. *Write out that check and subtract it from the checking account balance.* (**3C**)

Luckily, your boyfriend gets paid every Friday. *Deposit a week's check* (that would be *net pay*). (**4D**) Be sure to
check your figures.

Now you need to get your gas and electricity (PG&E)
hooked up. They tell you about the $150 deposit that will
be refunded at the end of a year if you pay all your bills on
time. Luckily, you still have enough in your checking
account. *Write a check to PG&E for the deposit.* (**5C**)

You need a phone. You learn that, because of your low income, you qualify for the LifeLine rate, so you only need to pay $35 for installation and then a monthly fee of $12.50 for local calls. *Write Pacific Bell a check for installation and one month's rate.* (**6C**)

Since your folks gave you a nice color TV last year, you want cable. The monthly rate is now $32.50. *Write Viacom Cablevision a check.* (**7C**) Gee, isn't it fun to spend money!

Your cute little duplex also needs the water turned on and you need trash pickup every week. The City of Napa charges you $26.00 for water and Napa Garbage Company needs $22.50. *Write checks to both.* (**8C, 9C**)

Your folks remind you to get renter's insurance which will cover your possessions in case your duplex burns down or you get flooded or robbed. You think that is unnecessary until your friend tells you about her friend who was left homeless after a fire — and had nothing for herself or her child. Pretty scary. So you call your mom's insurance agent and get $5,000 worth of coverage for $100 a year. *Write a check to State Farm for the full amount.* (**10C**)

You and your boyfriend are so happy to have a place of your own! You want to fix it up nice. You spend the weekend cleaning and scrubbing the floors, walls, refrigerator, and stove. You want things to be clean for your child.

Where Did All the Money Go?

Late Sunday afternoon you both are ready to go shopping for groceries. You don't qualify for food stamps because he makes too much money. Before you leave, you sit down together and write out menus for a week. He likes beef and you don't really care for it. He likes potatoes and you prefer rice. You both love fruit but there aren't too many vegetables you agree on.

After laughing a lot, you agree on five days of dinner

menus. Of course there is milk to buy, bread, and household items like toilet paper, paper towels, dishwashing soap, cleanser, light bulbs, ant traps, and toothpaste.

The bill at Safeway is $145.97. You about die! How could just a few bags of groceries add up to so much? *Write a check to Safeway, anyway.* **(11C)**

Your boyfriend asks how much is left and you tell him.

He waits until you are in the car to yell, **"Where did all that money go?"** Rather than get mad, you open the checkbook and show him all the bills that had to be paid. He calms down, but is moody the rest of the night.

The next week goes pretty well. Your child has trouble sleeping in the new room, but you are up only a few times during the night. You have fun planning what to do each day: What new thing to teach your child, what to make for dinner, what you would like to do with the living room.

Most of the meals you fix turn out okay, but you know you need to make more "from scratch" and not use so many mixes and boxes. The au gratin potatoes from a box tasted good but were very salty — you could make them yourself and regulate the salt. Also, you think the box is probably more expensive.

Fixing Up Your Home

On Friday, your partner comes home with his paycheck and *you deposit it.* **(12D)** What is your balance now?

Your second weekend together in your new place, your boyfriend decides to mow the lawn and you want to plant flowers. Payless has a sale on flowers. *Write a check for $15.88.* **(13C)** The neighbor has a lawnmower you can borrow.

You really want to put up nice curtains in the kitchen, bathroom, and bedrooms. You measure your windows and you all go to K-Mart and buy what you want. You like the pink and orange ones, he likes the blue and brown ones. You compromise by letting him pick the bedroom curtains and you pick out the others. The bill, including sales tax, comes to $45.67. *Write a check.* (**14C**)

You want a rug for the front room that's on sale at K-Mart for only $39. The two of you sit down at the snack bar and figure out the check balance. You can afford it, right? So why not buy it now? *Write a check for $41.92.* (**15C**)

2 A.M. — and Reality Strikes

Monday night at 2 A.M., you wake up with the realization that the rent has to be paid in three weeks and you haven't thought about saving up for it! You stay up for two hours figuring how to get enough money. You decide to use the entire amount of the next two paychecks plus take the rest from your checking account. If the rent is $695, how much will you have to subtract from your account? *Write one check for that amount to "Cash" right now,* just so you don't spend it. (**16C**) Put the check in an envelope marked "Rent."

Good grief! That leaves about $45 to live on for the rest of the month. You should never have bought the rug and you should have bought curtains one room at a time and one paycheck at a time.

From now on, you promise yourself, you will take one-fourth of the rent out of each week's paycheck, put it into the rent envelope, and hide it under your mattress. That way, you will have rent money when it's due and you will have money to spend every week. How much will you need to take out each week for the rent? (**17**) How much will you get to deposit into your checking account? (**18**)

When your boyfriend wakes up, you tell him about having to save every cent from now on. He grumbles about how every dime he makes disappears, but he kisses you good-bye as he leaves for work.

On Tuesday, you take your child and go shopping for groceries. You buy sugar, flour, baking powder, baking soda, spices (how can cinnamon cost $2.45 a jar??), and apples, and you vow to start cooking right.

You also buy three pounds of hamburger, broccoli, carrots, and canned tuna — and baby food (expensive!) No more boxed food. Less canned food. More fresh food — which is actually cheaper — but how in the world do you fix broccoli? You decide to check out the cookbook your mother gave you.

The bill at Safeway is $32.44. *Write a check.* **(19C)** The thought hits you that it isn't so much fun to spend money when you know you should be saving every cent. But you have to buy food.

Can You Afford to Entertain?

Your best friend and her boyfriend have been hinting that they'd like to come over for dinner — but you panic at the thought of having to feed two more people. Maybe macaroni and cheese would be cheap. But what about the dessert? That money *has* to go for the rent. Your friends will have to wait until you're in better shape financially. Or maybe *they* could bring dinner.

You fix lunch for yourself and your child — grilled cheese sandwiches, cooked carrots, and bananas. You promise to read to your child after lunch. She chooses two books you checked out from the library.

Your boyfriend has been trying to make extra money so he agreed to work overtime this week. *Deposit his extra $50 check.* **(20D)** Maybe you can make the money last this month after all.

You don't want to write a check each week for one-fourth of the rent, but how can you take this money out?

You remember your teacher telling you to use envelopes for each bill. You know it's risky to leave money lying around, so you decide to store your rent envelope in a frozen food container and stick it in your freezer. Good idea!

The Tidee Didee bill arrives, $55 for a month. You love getting clean, fresh diapers each week. *Write out a check to Tidee Didee.* (**21C**)

Back to K-Mart

You know you can't get by with what's left in your checking account. As much as it breaks your heart, you take down the curtains and return them to K-Mart. You get your money back and *deposit it into your account.* (**22D**)

How can you live for the next two weeks on what is left? What can be cut? If you hadn't walked on the rug, you would return that, too. Is this what they mean by "the working poor"? Sure, your boyfriend works, but it looks like your little family is on the poverty line.

When your boyfriend comes home, he asks about the missing curtains. You tell him what you did and why. The two of you sit down and try to work out what to do. You show him how you figured things out and he agrees with you. Money is very tight. He calls a friend about a job on Saturday. He can make $50 if he helps someone else move. Fifty dollars will help a lot.

On Wednesday, Planned Parenthood calls and reminds you to come in for your Depo-Provera shot. You make an appointment for next week knowing that the last thing you need is to get pregnant again. You fix lunch for yourself and your child — peanut butter sandwiches and peaches.

After lunch you call a friend, but she's busy and can't talk. You take your child for a walk around the neighborhood. The ice cream truck rolls by and you stop yourself from buying even that — you need to save money.

Your Entire Paycheck Goes to Rent

On Friday, your partner brings home his paycheck. You put the entire check, uncashed, in the envelope with the other money. Nothing goes into your checking account, but at least you know the rent money is there. You fix hamburgers, potato salad, and carrot sticks with chocolate cake for dessert. Your partner thanks you for such a great dinner.

Saturday you have dinner with his folks, and Sunday, with your folks. That helps on the food budget. When your mom asks how things are going, you say, "Fine!" Did she ever have trouble making ends meet, you wonder. Don't forget to *deposit the $50 your boyfriend earned into your checking account.* **(23D)**

Monday, you take your child for shots. Good thing you have medical insurance through your boyfriend's work. He put your child on his policy, but since you aren't his wife, you aren't covered. Luckily, your mom still carries you on her policy. Insurance is a big help — the bill was $85. Wow! So many expenses!

Eating Well on Little Money

When you get home, you try to plan meals for the next week using just what you have left. It looks like there will be lots of spaghetti, macaroni, noodles, and rice meals. What can you do to make them good? Macaroni and cheese works, but how much cheese do you have? Better get some. Put it on the grocery list.

Noodles. Noodles and what? How about salad dressing? You have Italian and Ranch dressing. Steam some carrots, onions, and broccoli, toss them with Italian dressing and serve on noodles. That's what they do in a fancy restaurant.

Spaghetti and sauce — that's easy — but how about adding hamburger meat from the freezer to the sauce? You'll need to plan time to thaw the meat before you cook it. So, the only thing you need is cheese. Wait until later in the week to go to the store — then you can get cheese and whatever else you need. Tonight, you'll have spaghetti.

For dessert, you can use up the spice cake mix and sprinkle a little powdered sugar on top in the shape of a heart — let your boyfriend know you appreciate him.

Back to the Supermarket

By Thursday, you need cheese, milk, eggs, and cereal. At the store, you notice that cereal is really expensive. Okay, no cereal. You'll have hot oatmeal for breakfast — it's healthy, it's cheap, and it's good with brown sugar in it. You add brown sugar to your list. You add up everything before you get to the checkout line:

Milk	3.39	Oatmeal	1.10
Eggs	1.89	Brown sugar	.89
Cheese	6.25		

There is no tax on food items. What is the total? *Write a check to Safeway for the total amount.* (**24C**)

Friday, thank goodness, and another paycheck. You stash that one with the other one in the envelope. Now you have enough to pay the rent next Wednesday. Can you make it 'til next Friday on what is left in your checking account?

Fitting in Some Fun

Your partner asks for gas money for the car. You stop at the bank, and you try not to panic as *you write a check to Cash for $40.* (**25C**) Good thing he works so close by — if you had $50 a month gasoline bills, what would you do? He asks if you would like to come along so you pack up your child in the car seat and go for a ride.

Saturday, the two of you stay home, watch TV, and play with your child. On Sunday, you pack a picnic lunch:

sandwiches, homemade cookies, apples, and milk in a
thermos and head for the park. Your child loves the swings,
and you take turns pushing for an hour.

On the way home, the ice cream truck goes by and your
partner buys $3 worth of goodies for all of you. He had
money left over from getting the car filled up with gas. You
feel happy with your life — if only it weren't for all those
bills and not enough money to buy things you want.

Entertaining Your Child at the Laundromat

On Monday, you do laundry, so you take your partner to
work so you can have the car. You stop at the bank, *write a
check to Cash for $20* (**26C**), and get quarters for the
machines.

In order to amuse your child for two hours at the
laundromat, you take along lots of books and spend your
time reading. Another young parent is there with two
children who just run wild. You are glad that you thought
ahead and planned what to do with your child.

That night, you plan to fix noodles and canned chow
mein. It isn't really wonderful and you are craving a hamburger from Wendy's. You have $14 left over from laundry
that you should save, but you and your boyfriend bundle up
your child and head for the nearest fast-food place for the
biggest cheeseburgers they have. And milk shakes. So you
now have $6 left from the original $20. Make it last!

Your Bank Statement Arrives

Your first bank statement arrives in the mail. When you
show it to your boyfriend, he's surprised to see the bank
appears to say you have more money than you show on
your check register.

Explain to him that not all the checks have been cashed.
Those outstanding (uncashed) checks must be considered

as you reconcile your bank statement. *Reconcile your register and bank statement.* Directions for this task are on page 108. Remember to deduct the $7 bank charge. **(27)**

This statement covers Month One.			
Summary	**Checks/Withdrawals**		**Deposits**
Previous	3C 1295.00	11C 145.97	4D 269.70
balance 1585.84	5C 150.00	13C 15.88	12D 269.70
Deposits 685.07	6C 47.50	14C 45.67	20D 50.00
Withdrawals 2010.38	7C 32.50	15C 41.92	22D 45.67
Service charge 7.00	8C 26.00	19C 32.44	23D 50.00
New Balance 253.53	9C 22.50	21C 55.00	
	10C 100.00		

Finding the Food Sales

Tuesday. Why not go shopping for groceries to last the rest of the week? You get the paper and check out food sales and clip coupons. Safeway has the cheapest chicken plus a special on carrots and potatoes. You also need bread from the day-old bread store. Their prices are great.

So you get out the stroller and head off to shop. First you hit the bread store. You notice that on Wednesdays, they have half-price day. So you only buy two loaves of bread for $1.50 and make a mental note to shop there only on Wednesdays.

You have $4.50 left in your purse. Now off to Safeway. The chickens look pink and fresh so you buy two: one to cook tonight and one to freeze for later. Your bill includes:

2 chickens	$3.99 *each*	Eggs	1.89
Milk	3.39	Carrots	2.29
Margarine	.89	Potatoes	1.99
Cheese	3.75	Onions	1.99

Write a check to Safeway for the total. **(28C)**

When you get home, your child is asleep. You put all the groceries away and look for a good chicken recipe to make for tonight. You decide to roast it with carrots and potatoes.

You season the chicken, wash and cut the vegetables, put everything in a roasting pan, and then lie down for a nap. Your child wakes up an hour later and you play for awhile. Then you start dinner, knowing it will take an hour to cook.

Togetherness at Home

When your boyfriend gets home, you have a wonderful dinner almost ready. He bathes the baby and puts her to bed while you do the dishes and get the kitchen cleaned up.

After dinner, you have some time to yourselves and you're so glad you're getting those Depo-Provera shots. Another child would be just too expensive! Think of the extra food, the extra diapers, the extra laundry, the extra everything. Whoever said two kids were no more expensive than one must have been a dreamer!

Wednesday. A friend who has a child older than yours calls and asks if you'd like to walk around downtown. You agree to meet her at Mervyn's. The two of you talk about your children, and she offers to give you all her child's clothes as they are outgrown. You never thought you'd let your child wear hand-me-down clothes, but after looking at the prices of kids' clothes in Mervyn's, you change your mind. You accept her offer gratefully.

You send Ms. Amador the rent money by going to the post office and getting a money order for the exact amount: $695. Do not subtract that from your checking account since the money came from your envelope at home.

Thursday. One more day until payday! You borrow the *Napa Valley Register* from a neighbor just to have something to read, and see a really cute shirt you want that's on sale at Mervyn's. You remember back to a time when you would have just asked your mom for money and she would have grumbled, but she would have given it to you. Now you have to account for every cent.

You wonder if it will always be like this. Your partner has been working for more than a year and hasn't had a raise, so maybe he will get one soon. But maybe not. Maybe he'll have to get a better job. Or maybe you'll have to go to work. Daycare is expensive, and you're going back to school this fall. Thank goodness for daycare at school. Who else would watch your child for free?

Today you clean the closets while your child sleeps. You take the chicken left over from last night and boil it with some white beans, more potatoes and carrots, plus some onions. The soup you make is really delicious. You serve it with bread, salad, and crackers. Dessert is cherry jello.

Payday — Remember the Rent!

Friday! Payday! You and your partner go to the bank to cash his check. You're determined to save the right amount from each check in order to pay the rent without having to worry about it. So, from the $269.70 he brings home, you take one-fourth of the rent money out and put it in the rent envelope. How much is left? *Deposit the remaining amount into your checking account.* (**29D**)

You also have to save for the same regular bills every month: diaper service, utilities, phone, cable, etc. Not to mention food, shampoo, tampons, gasoline. Maybe you should pay one or two bills out of every paycheck?

On the first of the month, most bills are due. You and your boyfriend decide which ones to pay early in the month, which ones to pay later. Some bills have a due date, and you will have to pay a fine or finance charge if you don't pay by then. You can't afford to pay any more money so you are careful to pay on time.

During the first week, *you pay last month's PG&E bill,*
$44.78. **(30C)** You promise yourself that you will make
sure all the lights are turned off and you don't leave the TV
on when nobody is watching it. Geez! Are you sounding
just like a parent?

Pacific Bell's bill is $12.50 since you didn't make any
long distance calls. Good thing you didn't call your girlfriend in San Diego. That would have cost about $5 more.
Write a check to Pacific Bell. **(31C)**

If you pay the diaper service now, you'll be overdrawn
for the rest of the week. Better wait on that one. *You pay*
Viacom Cable $32.50 and wonder if it's worth it. **(32C)**

You take your child to the park one day, to the library the
next. She loves to have you push her in her stroller. When
she falls asleep, you head for home so you can get some
housework done.

You'd love to have a car of your own but you couldn't
afford the gas or insurance even if someone *gave* you a car.

Your boyfriend calls you at lunch and says he can earn
extra money if he works late tonight. Even though you
don't like to be alone at night, you decide the money is
more important than your fears. He comes home at 10 P.M.
with $50 cash. *You deposit it the next day.* **(33D)**

Planning Those Daily Meals

On Tuesday, you're running out of groceries and ideas
for meals. Your mom has given you recipe books, but they
all look so hard. You never thought living with your boyfriend meant cooking and cleaning so much. Bor-ing! But it
has to be done and he is gone all day. You actually look
forward to school starting next month.

You decide that now your work is running the house so
you pull some recipe books off the shelf and write down
five dinner ideas. When your child wakes up from her nap,

you stroll down to Safeway and buy a bag of rice, a bag of black beans, a package of tortillas, more cheese, taco sauce, apples, bananas, milk, and orange juice. The total comes to $32.85. *Write a check to Safeway.* **(34C)**

You have never fed your child baby food. She started out on baby cereals, and you learned that if you mashed up fresh fruit and cooked vegetables, she liked that better than baby food. She still nurses several times a day so that helps out a lot with the food budget. You wonder how you could afford baby food at 54¢ per jar.

Your dinner menus are successful. The burritos are delicious. The next day you make rice pudding to go with the cheese sandwiches. On Wednesday, you take your child in her stroller to the day-old bread store and stock up on healthy grain breads, cornbread, English muffins, and even a chocolate cake. *Write a check to Growheat Bakery for $9.95.* **(35C)**

You make chili that night and serve hot cornbread. You tell your partner about how you saved money by using the bread store bargains. He loves the chocolate cake, but you have only a tiny piece since you don't want to pass caffeine to your baby and give her a stomach ache.

Payday — And the Bills Continue

Payday comes and you cash his check, keeping out the rent part, then *deposit what's left.* **(36D)** How much did you deposit? What is your bank balance now?

You have enough now to pay more bills. *Write a check to Tidee Didee for $55.* **(37C)** You'd like to go back to K-Mart and buy those curtains, but you're afraid some other expense might come up. On Saturday, when you're at the Goodwill store, you find a set of kitchen curtains that are perfect for only $5. *Write a check.* **(38C)**

Your partner needs a set of tires for the car so *he writes a* *check to his friend, Jose Ortiz, for $40.* (**39C**) That makes you very nervous, but you know the car needs tires. But it's another whole week before payday!

Money-Talk Again

During the next week, your partner needs gas for the car. He asks for $15 but all you can afford is $5. You go to the bank together to *write a check to Cash for $5* (**40C**) and have to face the fact that you have only $4.56 left in your checking account after this last check is cashed.

"Where does the money go?" he asks. That night, you sit down again and talk about all the bills and expenses. Is there any way to cut down more? Can you do anything to make some extra money? You don't have much time to devote to a new project because you have a full-time job taking care of your child and doing the shopping, cleaning, cooking, and paying attention to what needs to be done.

Sometimes it bothers you that all your boyfriend does is go to his work and come home. He doesn't think about all the bills or if the baby is eating or sick. He just does his thing and expects everything else to fall into place.

He's Always with His Friends

It's starting to get on your nerves that he and his friends work on cars every Saturday afternoon. You want to do things as a family but he says his buddies need him. He says he's with you every night, and that should be enough.

What about your friends? Your best friend graduated and went to live with her aunt and go to college. Another friend never goes anywhere unless her boyfriend takes her. You'd like to have someone just to hang out with, maybe share recipes, go window shopping. Something!

While he's with his friends, you go with your child to the library and look at picture books. That night you make spaghetti without meatballs since you don't have ground meat. You serve chocolate cake and ice cream for dessert.

On Tuesday you and your child go for a walk. You'd like to have a bus pass, but you can't afford it. Lucky for you, the weather is nice.

That night you make au gratin potatoes for dinner from scratch. They are delicious, but your boyfriend asks why there isn't any meat with dinner. You have to say because there is only a little left in your checking account.

Mom Helps Out

Wednesday, your mom calls and invites you to go to Costco with her. She offers to buy you some groceries if you need them. You jump at the chance. She buys you frozen hamburger patties, frozen chicken breasts, orange juice, cheese, a cherry pie, a jar of spaghetti sauce, and a box of noodles. You both laugh at how she used to buy you clothes, but now it's food. How your life has changed!

That night you make chicken-rice casserole and serve the pie. Thank goodness for your mom!

Thursday you and your child go do laundry at your mom's house which saves you lots of money. You use your mom's soap and bleach. You tell your mom how hard it is to make ends meet and how much you appreciate the help. You never thought you'd be thanking your mom for letting you do laundry.

That night, you fix hamburger, onions, potatoes, and green pepper in a casserole. It's great with melted cheese on top, and you have the last of the pie for dessert. Your boyfriend says he loves your cooking.

Will It Ever Get Better?

Two weeks go by. You take money out for rent, plus $10 cash each time. *You deposit all that's left after the rent and*

the cash. **(41D, 42D)** You have money to pay your bills —
City of Napa (water), $26.00 **(43C)** and Napa Garbage,
$22.50. **(44C)** You shop for two weeks' supply of food at
Safeway, and the bill totals $78.90. **(45C)** *Write the checks.*

Your bank statement arrives. *Reconcile the statement
and register.* Note the $7 service charge. **(46)**

This statement covers Month Two.						
Summary		**Checks/Withdrawals**			**Deposits**	
Previous		16C 155.60	31C 12.50		29D 95.95	
balance	253.53	24C 13.52	32C 32.50		33D 50.00	
Deposits	413.80	25C 40.00	34C 32.85		36D 95.95	
Withdrawals	466.87	26C 20.00	35C 9.95		41D 85.95	
Service charge	7.00	28C 24.17	37C 55.00		42D 85.95	
New Balance	**193.46**	30C 44.78	43C 26.00			

You've been living together now for two months. You
think of the rest of your life being like this. How will you
have money for Christmas or holiday gifts? What about
your birthday coming up — will your boyfriend buy you
something nice? How can he afford it?

You used to think it was so wonderful when a guy
bought his girl a diamond ring. Now you'd think he was
stupid for spending all that money when it could go for
food or laundry or gasoline for the car.

Over the weekend, he works on his car at his friend's
house while you make chicken stew and biscuits for dinner.
He calls to tell you he will be late and will eat with his
friend. Will you save the chicken stew and biscuits for
tomorrow night? If you do, what will you fix tonight for
you and your child?

Budgeting by the *Year*

On Monday, in the mail, comes a notice about car insurance. It is due in a month. The premium is $350, and that's

only for three months. When your partner gets home, you're upset and crying. He says he'll get another job on the weekends, but that makes you cry harder because you think you'll never see him.

The two of you sit down and write out a budget, not just for a month, but for a year so there will be no surprises like this car insurance. With all the expenses just as they are — no increases — the amount of money you can spend on food and household expenses each week is even smaller: $70.22.

You wanted to get a perm. You wanted to get your baby's pictures taken. You wanted new towels for the bathroom and curtains for the bedroom. You don't want to be poor forever!

Saving for Emergencies

Your partner reminds you that you've been figuring four paychecks per month. Actually, there are 52 weeks in the year, not 48. What about those extra four paychecks? Shouldn't that be added to your annual budget?

You talk about it, and agree that would be nice. But then you think — What if the rent goes up? What if your partner gets sick and can't work? What if his car breaks down? You really need a savings account. You agree that each time you have five paychecks in one month, you'll put a big share of that fifth paycheck in a savings account. That's the only way you'll ever get things for your apartment, or a different car, or clothes . . .

This acting-like-an-adult stuff is really hard, and love doesn't pay the bills.

Welcome to the real world!

Your child loves to read with you.

CHAPTER 3

Two Moms, Two Toddlers

You've been living with your mom since you were born and now your own child is two years old. How can you be only 18 when you feel so much older? Your mom has been hinting that maybe it's time for you to look for a place of your own.

Since your ex-boyfriend doesn't seem interested in asking you to marry him, you've been thinking that you and a girl you met in the Teen Moms class, Renee, might get a place together. The two of you get along great and your kids like each other. It just might work out.

You and Renee look in the paper and find some two-bedroom apartments that cost between $650 and $750 per month. Of course, you would be paying only half of that which would be a lot easier than paying the whole amount.

You look at a few places and really like a cute ground-floor apartment with a nice back yard off the kitchen so you can cook and watch the kids from the window. The bed-rooms are both large enough for a bed for you and your child plus some furniture. It has big closets for storage, and the best part is a washer and dryer in the apartment. Wow! All that for only $725!

Can You Afford It?

But can you afford it? That's the big question. Keep reading.

You each work a total of 24 hours a week with no ben-efits like health insurance, but at least you have jobs. You make $6.50 per hour and Renee makes $6.75. *Figure out what you make, before taxes, in a four-week month.* **(1)**

What does Renee make, before taxes, during the same time period? **(2)**

Of course you don't get to keep all that money — you have to pay taxes. That money is taken out before you even see it. Multiply your monthly wage by .13 (13 percent), subtract that amount, which is your tax, and the remainder is the amount you really get to take home for paying bills. *What is your amount?* **(3)**

What is Renee's? **(4)**

Now, *what is your total household income?* **(5)**

If you are paying $725 just in rent, what will you use to buy food, pay for water, garbage, utilities like heat and lights, a phone? Back to the drawing board. That apartment is too expensive for your little family unit.

In the paper, you see duplexes for less money each month. You're not sure what a duplex is until your aunt explains that it's two apartments side by side. Sometimes it looks like just one place but is divided into two units.

You and Renee go looking, and you find a two-bedroom

unit in an old house. It has a large front room, a huge kitchen and dining area, and the bedrooms and bath are upstairs. You worry about the kids falling down the stairs and decide to keep looking.

You Find Your Apartment

Another duplex is a back unit, near the bus line, with a yard, trees, and a clothesline so you can save money by not using a dryer. It's $600 a month, and is just like a little house. The rooms are small but clean, and you like the neighborhood. It feels safe.

The owner lives in the front of the property and she tells you there are no overnight guests allowed — like your boyfriends can't stay over. (As if you had one.) You're not sure it's legal for her to have that rule, but you like the place and ask for an application.

She also tells you about the $500 deposit, which is refundable if you leave the place as clean as it is now. That's a total of $1100 up front to move in. And the question again is: Can you afford it? You have $500 saved and Renee has the same amount. If you both put money into one account for the household expenses every week from your paychecks, you can probably afford it. Time to get your checkbook organized:

Deposit $500 from your bank into your new account. Deposit $500 from Renee's bank into the same account. **(6D)** Since you are still waiting to be approved for the duplex, you have a week to make more money. At the end of the week, you *deposit half of your paycheck.* (You will need to divide your monthly salary by four to get the weekly amount, then figure half of that.) **(7D)** Just to make everything fair, *Renee deposits the exact same amount.* **(8D)**

Add those deposits to the amount you already put in

your account. *Do you have enough money now for the duplex?* **(9)**

What would you have left over if you paid for the rent and the deposit? **(10)**

You both decide to wait another week and save even more. The next week, you decide to deposit a bit more money. *So you put in $65 and so does Renee.* **(11D)** *What is your balance now?* **(12)**

Mrs. Amad calls you with the news that the duplex is yours if you want it, and if you write her a check for the full $1100 now. You get your mom to drive you over and *you write the check.* **(13C)** It is your first check from your new account! This is exciting!

One of the best parts of having a roommate is that you can share childcare. When you work Tuesday through Friday from 4-10 p.m., Renee can watch both kids. When she goes to work on weekends from 6 a.m. to 6 p.m., you can watch them. That way, neither of you has to pay for childcare and the kids can stay in their own home. All of your money can go toward rent and household expenses.

Moving In

On Monday, you and Renee and your kids start to move in. It takes more than one day because you have to wait for your cousin who has a truck to help with the big stuff, plus you have to work every day at 4 p.m., but you and Renee do most of the moving.

You take a hot bath that night to soothe your tired muscles, while Renee boils some spaghetti and mixes butter with garlic powder. When you get out, you spread French bread with the seasoned butter and pour hot spaghetti sauce on the pasta. Dinner is served.

Renee gives the kids a bath while you clean up after dinner. Teamwork is so important.

Mrs. Amad told you to sign up for utilities in your own name since she will have it shut off in hers. Look in the phone book and find the 800 number for Pacific Gas and Electric. *What is it?* **(14)**

When you call, they ask you a ton of questions about your income, your marital status, number of kids, your credit cards, your rent.

You discover that you will have to pay a deposit based on what the bill for your little apartment has been in the past. The people who lived there before you were very careful and didn't waste electricity and gas, so you only have to pay a deposit of $60. Luckily, you have that much in your account. *Write a check to PG&E* **(15C)**, and write their number down on your **Important Phone Numbers** page. You might need to call them in the future, now that you are a customer.

Now you need a phone. *Find the 800 number for Pacific Bell's Residential Customer Service.* **(16)** Write that number down on your Phone Numbers list so you will have it in case of a problem.

When you call, you find out that you have to pay an installation fee of $40. Luckily, you still have money in that bank account, so *write a check to Pacific Bell.* **(17C)** You were able to keep the cost down because you and Renee agreed not to get any special calling features.

Pacific Bell charges for every little extra and over a twelve-month period of time, it adds up. Just $2.50 per month would mean $30 wasted in a year. That's money you could have saved for medicine or a special trip with your child. As it is, the monthly charge will be $12.87 as long as you don't make any long-distance or toll calls.

It's Friday. Pay Day. You and Renee get your paychecks. This time, you both put in even more money: *deposit $75 each.* **(18D)** Add that to your checking account balance.

Your New Life

Renee works Saturday and Sunday from 6 a.m. until 6 p.m. so you have both kids all day. You make them oatmeal for breakfast. Then you all go for a short walk outside to find leaves. When you come back, you let them watch Sesame Street (Renee has a TV) while you clean up the kitchen, put dirty clothes in the washing machine (and discover you don't have any laundry soap!), make beds, and think about a grocery list. What to fix for the next few meals?

The kitchen cupboards are pretty bare and you need to buy groceries. On Monday morning, your day off, you and Renee pack up the kids and walk to Safeway. You buy laundry soap, flour, sugar, cinnamon, cereal, milk, bananas, frozen orange juice, a whole fresh chicken, potatoes, onions, carrots, tortillas, beans, rice, bread, and no junk food or candy. The total is $51.76. *Write a check to Safeway.* (**19C**)

You go home, and while Renee reads to the kids, you boil the chicken with a cut-up onion for flavor. You also boil some beans, cook a big pot of rice, and put soap in the washing machine.

For lunch, the kids eat some crackers and cheese with a sliced banana, but dinner tonight is chicken burritos. They're good except you forgot to buy hot sauce. You use some sauce left over from Taco Bell, and you decide you'd better start a **Shopping List**. Write down cheese, green sauce, tomato sauce, and chicken broth.

After dinner, you and Renee let the kids color on the brown bags you got from Safeway. You want always to do one fun thing with your child every day.

The next day, you feed the kids cold cereal and make yourselves tea and toast. You forgot to buy margarine. Put it on your **Shopping List #1**. Add jelly, too. Oh and don't forget the peanut butter. Your child has been asking for it — peebubba — but you know what that means.

Paying Less for Food

You've heard about a place on Third Street that sells bread and pastry products for less money. They have even lower prices on Wednesday. After spending over $3.00 for a loaf of good bread at Safeway, you and Renee take the kids in their strollers and walk to the bread store where you find good, hearty bread, French rolls, bread sticks for the kids, cheese crackers, low fat oatmeal/raisin cookies, and pizza crusts. You pile up your purchases on the strollers, *write a check to Orowheat Bakery for $12.69* (**20C**), and head for home, loaves of bread falling off now and then.

By the time you get home with your bruised bread, you and Renee are laughing and planning to get a wagon or something. While you fix lunch of chicken burritos, Renee puts everything away. After the kids have a nap, you all go to the store again and buy all the things on **Shopping List #1**. *Write a check to Albertson's for the total which you'll have to figure out.* (**21C**)

Tomato sauce 1.00 Chicken broth 1.00	Peanut butter 2.69 Cheese 5.99 Green sauce 1.99	Margarine 1.79 Strawberry jam 2.79

Renee fixes dinner that night — bean, rice, and cheese burritos with green sauce. Much better! They even have oatmeal cookies and milk for dessert. You eat when you get home from work.

Next day you make chicken soup out of what is left of the chicken by adding potatoes, carrots, rice, and more onions, then letting it all simmer for two hours. That makes dinner for two nights along with toasted French rolls. It isn't fancy food but it's good. Write down on **Shopping List #2:** spaghetti sauce, spaghetti, macaroni, noodles, celery, and garlic powder.

Since you don't have a VCR, you can't rent videos for

the kids to watch, and that's just fine with you because you like to **Do Things** with your kids. You finger-paint, you make hand impressions with the paint on paper plates and save them to mail to your grandparents (at the moment, you don't have any stamps), you outline the kids' bodies on the back patio and let them use washable chalk to color in clothes, hair, and faces. They mostly scribble but that's okay — it was fun for all of you to play together. Put "stamps" on your **Shopping List #2**.

Your Bank Statement Arrives

Before you go to work, you and Renee reconcile your check register and bank statement. Be sure to include your outstanding checks and to deduct the check charge. **(22C)**.

This statement covers Month One.			
Summary	Checks/Withdrawals		Deposits
Previous balance 00.00	13C 1100.00		1D 1000.00
Deposits 1415.72	15C 60.00		7D 67.86
Withdrawals 1264.45	17C 40.00		8D 67.86
Check charge 8.00	19C 51.76		11D 130.00
New Balance **143.27**	20C 12.69		18D 150.00

Pay Day again. You and Renee decide to stay with the plan of depositing $75 each. *Put that in your account.* **(23D)** For you, that means having only $60.72 for the week just for yourself. Since the household checking account is paying for almost everything else, you get along fine. You buy shampoo, nail polish, and make-up with your own money, plus you also buy your child's clothes and diapers. You haven't bought clothes for yourself in so long, you can't remember. There never seems to be any extra money.

Finding the Rent Money

Saturday morning you're home with both kids and Renee is at work when you remember. We have to pay the

rent in two weeks! Do we have the money? The rent is
$600. How much do you have in the checking account?
You get out a pencil and paper and do some figuring. You
have $276.02 now. You have two more paydays until the
rent is due. If you each put in $75 each pay day, that will
give you $300 more. *Will you be able to pay the rent?* (**24**)
Your mind is whizzing. How can you spend less on food?
Where can you cut back? How can you get more money
into your checking account in the next two weeks?

Well, of course, you and Renee will have to put *all* your
paychecks into the account. That might fix it, you think.
Time to refigure: Okay, *you now have* (**25**) *in the checking
account.*

Next Pay Day: *(add in the entire weekly paycheck)*
Renee. You.

Week after next: *Renee. You.*

GRAND TOTAL (**26**)

Now, *can you pay the rent?* (**27**)

When Renee comes home, you tell her what you figured
out. She sees that you both need to figure out a way to save
for the rent out of each week's paycheck. If each of you
pays $300, which is half the rent, how about each of you
saving one-fourth of that amount each week before putting
money into the checking account. *How much would each of
you be saving each week toward the rent?* (**28**) Okay. So
next month, you will start that system. For now, you just
need to put all of your paychecks in the checking account.

You settle into a routine. During the weekdays, you and
Renee spend lots of time with the kids. You go to the park,
you go for walks (always taking the strollers because your
kids get tired easily), you let them help you clean the
house, they dance to music on the radio, and you teach
them silly songs.

You go to work at 4 p.m., and the kids are asleep when

you get home. Your child doesn't wake up when you come
in most of the time, but you are always there in the morning. It's nice. Renee works all weekend and that gets a little
hard for you — to be the mom for what seems like twins —
but she shares the work when she gets home in the evening.

You and Renee — A Team

Friday arrives. Pay Day again. You know you have to put
your entire check in the household account, so go ahead
and *deposit all of your and all of Renee's weekly check.*
(29D) (You figured this out at the beginning of the story.
Check with your teacher if you're not sure you're right.)
That means no extra money for that cute shirt you saw at
Wal-Mart.

Renee points out that her share is more than yours but
since it's kind of an emergency, she agrees to do it. You feel
bad that you aren't able to contribute as much as she does,
so you offer to clean the refrigerator. She laughs and says,
"Go ahead." If your mom could see you now she'd be
amazed because you used to hate to clean the refrigerator,
and here you are volunteering. You're really behaving like
an adult!

You hate taking the garbage out. You ask Renee if she's
willing to take it out most of the time. She says sure, as
long as you agree to clean the toilet, which she really hates
to do. Trading garbage duty for toilet duty seems fair and
you both feel good about the deal.

Daytimes are busy. There are things to get done around
the house, cleaning, cooking, ironing, and thinking of
things to amuse the kids. You let them jump on your mattress since it's on the floor anyway and they can't break the
springs. You paint their faces with butterflies and their arms
with ivy and they pretend to be birds. You drape blankets
and sheets over the table and they make a fort. They love to

dance to radio music — you keep it on a station that plays oldies or country — none of that awful stuff for your child's ears!

Even though the rent is due soon, you need to buy more groceries. Take the kids to Safeway and buy everything on your shopping list #2. *Write a check for the total* (**30C**):

Spaghetti sauce 2.99	Spaghetti 1.99	Celery .99
Garlic powder 1.59	Macaroni 1.69	Stamps 6.80
	Noodles .69	

Dinner that night is spaghetti, no meatballs, but the sauce has mushrooms and it's really good. You spread some French rolls with margarine and garlic powder and broil them — yum!

Your most popular lunches are still peanut butter and jelly sandwiches — the kids love that — but you and Renee prefer cheese sandwiches and celery stuffed with peanut butter. You mostly drink water since cokes and Pepsi are so expensive, and you save the milk for the kids.

Time to Shop *Again*

While Renee cleans up the kitchen, she asks you to start **Shopping List #3**: cheese, tuna, ground turkey, kidney beans, cream of celery soup, cream of mushroom soup, crackers, milk, oatmeal, brown sugar, and tortillas. You'd love to get some ice cream or cookies, but the rent is due next week.

Breakfast is oatmeal for the kids and toast with jam for you and Renee. Usually whoever cleans up, gets to eat what the kids leave. Coffee is too expensive but you have some tea bags your mom gave you. You can't believe the price of boxed cereal — $4.69 for some of it! At lunchtime, you fix tortillas with grated cheese on top. Dinner that night is macaroni and cheese, which is good but uses up the last of the milk.

The next day you all pack up and go to Albertson's. Buy everything on your **Shopping List #3** plus other things you need — bananas, toilet paper, dish soap, paper towels, laundry soap. The total comes to $35.78. Write a check. **(31C)**

For lunch, you fix peanut butter sandwiches and sliced bananas. That night Renee makes a really wonderful tuna casserole. You eat it when you get home at 10:30 p.m.

Another payday! *Deposit both your checks.* **(32D)** Since the rent is due on Tuesday, go ahead and *write a check to Mrs. Amad for $600.* **(33C)**

That took a big chunk out of your checking account. You can see why some people your age are still living with their parents. Make a note of Mrs. Amad's phone number on your Important Phone Numbers list. It is 256-4456.

The PG&E bill arrives. *Write a check for $46.65* **(34C)**, which is based on what your family unit used last month. Make a mental note to turn off all lights when you leave a room. And stop holding the refrigerator door open. The phone bill is due also. It comes to $12.87. *Write a check to Pacific Bell.* **(35C)**

Your period starts and you don't have any tampons. Renee goes to Safeway for tampons and pain pills, and while she's there, she picks up a few things for the house: Drano, cleanser, light bulbs, and toilet paper. *She writes a check for $26.96.* **(36C)** Be sure to subtract it from your check register.

Your Child Gets Sick

Money is getting low again. Your child gets a cold. When you look up your doctor's number, you write it down on your Important Phone Numbers list. It is 256-7890. You know you don't have insurance, but you talk to the nurse who tells you to get some nose drops and some cough medicine.

You walk to the store while Renee watches both kids, and you *write a check to Safeway for $8.44.* (**37C**) When you get home, your child is crying for Popsicles and ice cream. You go to the store for the second time that day and buy those things plus you get some apple juice, Jell-O, applesauce, and 7-up. The total to Safeway this time is $9.56. *Write a check.* (**38C**)

While you are rocking your child and singing, the doorbell rings. A salesman wants to tell you about some vitamins that will make you and your family healthy. They cost $20 per month. That's a lot of money! You tell him no, thank you, and close the door. You know not to let anyone into the apartment.

The next day, your child is better but you're feeling sick. Of course, you have to go to work anyway. It's not like when you lived at home and your mom used to call the school for you and write absence notes and everything would be fine. Now, you have to show up or risk losing your job. You decide to call your employer anyway and tell him you're sick. The number is 265-2345 — make a note of it.

Your boss tells you that taking one day off would be okay but you would not get paid for it. You think about how close you came to not being able to pay the rent last month — on a full paycheck — and you decide you'd better go to work.

It's payday again. Renee wants to get a perm so she isn't going to put her full paycheck into the household account. She only puts in $100. You decide to put in the same. *Make your deposit.* (**39D**) Deduct from your checking account balance the $150 you need each week for the rent. (Don't write a check now because you'll do that at the end of the month when you pay Mrs. Amad.) How much money do you have to spend now? (**40**) With some money in the bank, you both sit down and make out **Shopping List #4**:

Bananas			
Peanut butter	Buttermilk	Eggs	Tuna
Jelly	Milk	Baking soda	Brown rice
Noodles	Sugar	Toilet paper	Flour
Green sauce	Tomato sauce	Cheese	Applesauce
Baking powder	Beans	Tomato soup	Dish soap

You spend half an hour clipping coupons from the
Safeway ad to save money. Then you both take the kids and
head for the store. You tell the kids what you need in each
aisle and they "help" you look. It gives them something to
do and you tell them how smart they are when they find
what you need. The total comes to $59.06. *Write a check to
Safeway.* **(41C)**

Renee Has a Dinner Guest

Renee has been talking to a guy a lot on the phone. She
tells you she wants to have him over some night for dinner.
You tell her to plan on having something cheap that night
because you can't afford to feed her boyfriend. She asks
you if you would take the kids to a movie for a few hours
that night. You say this place is our home, and if you want
to be with some guy, you need to do it away from here.

She's not too thrilled to hear you say that, but she agrees.

She invites the guy over for next Friday night. You will
be working until 10 p.m. anyway. When you get home, the
dishes are not cleaned up, the kitchen is a mess, and both
kids are asleep in your bed. Renee's door is closed, but you
can hear talking. You're feeling really upset. You can't go
to sleep because there's no room in your bed plus you're
worried about ants coming into the kitchen.

You finally fall asleep on the sofa, and the next morning
you wake up to Renee cleaning the kitchen and crying. She
tells you the guy left after midnight and said he'd call, but

she doesn't even want him to because he yelled at the kids when milk was spilled at dinner. She can see that he isn't good with children.

You tell her that you were worried that he might be a bad influence on your child. Did he smoke? Did he swear? Was he rude? You two talk about it for an hour and decide that you have to stick together to make this roommate situation work. Having him here was a big stress on you both. There is a new house rule: no guys for dinner. If a guy wants to get to know you, he can take you out.

You Think Ahead

That night in bed, listening to your child breathing, you think about your life up to this point. You are definitely "On Your Own," but you've also learned that living with other people means compromising. You can't just do whatever you want to do when you want to do it. You have your child and your roommate to consider also. It's a lot like having to think about what your mom or dad would think or say when you were living at home.

What if your child gets sick? Or you? You decide you need to open a savings account even if you can save only $5 a week. You're beginning to realize you need to work more hours or get a better paying job. You'll talk to your boss tonight.

Maybe being "On Your Own" means setting up a household that's pretty much like what any normal family life is like. There have to be schedules for getting chores done and keeping doctor appointments. There have to be rules for who can visit and how long they can stay. There have to be plans made for the future — like getting the rent paid. There have to be lists kept for telephone numbers and things to buy when you shop. You've discovered that life has to be organized! *And you've gotten much better at it.*

A baby means lots of expenses — along with the joy.

CHAPTER 4

You Are a Teen Dad

How can this be happening to you? You are 17, starting your senior year in high school. Your girlfriend tells you she's pregnant. She says the baby is due in three months.

So now what? You ask about abortion, but she says it's way too late, and besides, she wouldn't do that.

So you say, "Well, what are you going to do?"

She fires back, "You mean, what are *we* going to do? You're as responsible for this baby as I am. We're in this together."

You think, I suppose she's right. You two talk for awhile, and then you go home.

Two weeks later your girlfriend's mom calls your mom and tells her. Your mom is furious. "What do you think you're going to do now?" she screams.

You try to tell your mom you can help with the baby.
You can buy diapers and milk and stuff. She just snorts and
tells you, "It's called formula, and do you even know how
much diapers cost?"

She reminds you that she's done all the child-raising she
plans to do in her life, and so don't even think that she is
going to help take care of this child. "And just wait until I
tell your father," she says.

Welcome to the Real World

Great. All you need is another lecture. Your dad lives an
hour away with his girlfriend and her kids so he isn't going
to be much trouble — but he'll figure he has to yell at you
about it. Sure enough, he calls that night and tells you about
the District Attorney and child support.

You didn't know you can even go to jail if you don't pay
your share. Or you can have your wages attached. That
means they take money out for the kid before you ever get
your paycheck.

"Welcome to the real world, son," your dad says.

The job you have now, after school, pays $7 an hour.
You average 17 hours a week. After taxes, you take home
$97 each week. You thought this would support your car,
the few clothes you buy, and money for CDs and going out.
You thought you were all set for this last year of high
school. Will the baby change that, you wonder.

Your car insurance is due in two weeks — $197.50 for
three months. You've had your '71 VW Bug for a year, and
with your buddy's help, you've kept it running most of the
time. You only have the basic insurance, enough to stay
legal, but no collision. You can't afford it.

You realize you have to get serious about money. You've
got to get organized. Your mom goes with you to her bank
and you set up a checking account. Already you've saved

$269 from odd jobs during the summer.

You've got an uncashed check in your jacket pocket. Take $40 out for expenses (gas, going out with your buddies, seeing your girlfriend). *Deposit the remaining $57, along with the money from your savings.* (**1D**) You figure that's a pretty healthy bank account.

You take your girlfriend out to dinner so you can talk. You go to Sizzler and spend $19.60 of your $40 cash. On the way, you put gas in your car. That cost $11.35 cash.

Time to See the Doctor

Your girlfriend asks you to go with her to see her doctor next week. She's applied for Medi-Cal, but won't have her card for another month. She says she can't wait that long to see a doctor, that it would be dangerous for the baby if she doesn't start taking care of herself. You agree to go along, and you know you'll have to pay the doctor bill.

You deposit your weekly paycheck, but you're out of money so you take $50 in cash again. *Deposit the remaining $47.* (**2D**)

A week later you meet your girlfriend and take her to the doctor. She insists you stay with her while the doctor examines her, and you feel grown-up and weird at the same time. As you leave, the receptionist says the bill for today, including vitamins, is $85. *You write a check to Dr. Hauser.* (**3C**) Your girlfriend says she'll have her Medi-Cal card for her next appointment. That's a relief.

On the way home your girlfriend wants to stop at K-Mart and look at baby clothes. Together you pick out booties, two receiving blankets, and a couple of one-piece sleeper outfits. *You write a check for $37.65.* (**4C**) This is already getting expensive. It's a good thing you got a paycheck yesterday. You kept out only $20 cash this time. *Deposit the remaining $77.* (**5D**)

There was a crib at K-Mart you both liked, but it was $89. The car seat was $65. She said you have to have a car seat to take the baby home from the hospital — it's a law. Maybe next week you'll buy that.

Your paycheck was a little short this week ($85) since you had to take time off to go to the doctor with your girlfriend. You decide to get by on $10 cash this week. *Deposit $75.* **(6D)**

It's time to pay the car insurance bill. *Write the check to Blake Insurance Company for $197.50.* **(7C)**

At least you have enough for the car insurance this time. Of course that's only for three months, and you're lucky you got the cheapest rate because of your 3.0 grade average and your clean driving record. It's still a lot of money.

You're relieved to see you still have about $200 in your checking account, but your girlfriend reminds you that the baby, once it's born, is going to be expensive.

She also says she's cold and she doesn't have a sweater or sweatshirt that fits anymore. You stop at K-Mart and get an extra large zipper sweatshirt. You also get a cute little stretch sleeper for the baby. *Write a check for $37.45.* **(8C)** Your girlfriend thinks the little sleeper is cute. You mostly see dollar signs.

Advice from Your Buddies

Your buddies heard you're going to be a father. Jose tells you he's already a dad, but since he's only 17, he doesn't have to pay child support until later. He's never seen his child, and you think that's pretty lame. Buying things for the baby and your girlfriend makes you feel like an adult, like you matter to somebody besides yourself.

Mitch thinks you're crazy and that you should dump your girlfriend. He says the baby might not be yours — girls sometimes lie about who the father is just so they can get help with the expenses. You don't think your girlfriend had sex with anyone else, but you listen to Mitch talk about getting blood tests after the baby is born, just in case.

You and Mitch and Jose take a ride in Frank's car to pick up a new set of tires for his car. You say something about how you'd really like to have a better car. Jose jokes that you can't afford a good set of wheels because you have to buy a stroller for the baby. Everybody laughs except you.

Her Clothes Don't Fit

Your girlfriend is getting bigger all the time. She's depressed a lot these days. Frankly, you aren't having as much fun together as you were. You know she's stressed out, but so are you. You try to be reassuring when she gets in one of her moods.

She needs some maternity clothes because nothing fits her anymore. You go to Sears and she tries on several outfits. You buy her three tops and two pairs of stretch pants. She thinks she looks ugly but you think she looks cute — just pregnant.

Write a check for $81.14 to Sears. (**9C**) That's just about the total of what you made this week! *Deposit your regular check, $97.* (**10D**) You don't figure you can take cash out this time.

Your car needs some work, and your buddy comes over to help you. You don't need more expense right now, but you find you have to replace the carburetor. Your buddy helps you find one that's been rebuilt for $83. *Write the check to Karen's Repair Shop.* (**11C**) Almost another week's salary gone!

Reconciling Your Bank Statement

Your bank statement arrives and you figure out how to reconcile the bank's balance with the balance you have in your check register. You can't afford bounced checks, and if you don't keep careful track of that balance, it would be easy to write more checks than you have money.

One of your buddies wrote a check to Wal-Mart, and he didn't have money in his account to pay it. Wal-Mart charged him $15 extra and the bank charged him $12. You don't want that!

This statement covers Month One.						
Summary		**Checks/Withdrawals**			**Deposits**	
Previous balance	00.00	3C	85.00	8C	37.45	1D	326.00
Deposits	622.00	4C	37.65	11C	83.00	2D	47.00
Withdrawals	440.60	7C	197.50			5D	77.00
Check charge	8.50					6D	75.00
New Balance	**172.90**					10D	97.00

Enter in your check register the $8.50 check charge. **(12)** Subtract that from your balance. *Then reconcile your bank statement with your check register.*

Your girlfriend's aunt has a baby shower for her, and she gets some clothes for the baby and two boxes of diapers. You two go over what you still need before the baby is born. Yikes! You still need a crib, a car seat, and a stroller. You go back to K-Mart and get the car seat. The price is $65 plus 7 percent tax. *Write a check to K-Mart.* **(13C)**

You tell your girlfriend that's all you can afford today, and that you don't need the stroller for several months. Actually, that check just about wipes out your checking account balance. No movie this week, not even hamburgers for you and your girlfriend.

Recycling the Crib

But what about the crib? You need that right away. You and your girlfriend stop at your house to show your mom the new car seat and tell her you may be able to buy the crib in two more weeks. She suggests you use the crib in your garage, the one she bought you when you were a baby. You and your girlfriend think that's a great idea.

You get it down and clean it up so you'll be ready. The following Saturday you and your girlfriend go to the paint store and buy paint for the crib, making sure it's lead-free paint. You want your baby to stay healthy.

You also need a paint brush and some sandpaper. *Write a check to Vista Paint for $12.32.* **(14C)** You paint the crib while your girlfriend takes a nap. She's tired all the time these days.

Go to the bank and deposit this week's check, $97. **(15D)** No cash again this week. You're just relieved to see some money back in your account.

Your Girlfriend Moves In

Your girlfriend has been having a lot of trouble with her parents. She really wants to move out. The two of you have talked about getting your own place but you don't see how you can afford it.

She calls you one night, crying, and you decide to talk to your mom about letting your girlfriend move in with you. You're surprised when your mom calls her mom, and after that conversation, your mom agrees.

You kind of thought your mom would say no. But she didn't, and here you are, packing up half your clothes, tapes, shoes and *stuff* to make room for your girlfriend. You hope this works out okay.

You already sleep on a twin bed, and your mom is borrowing another twin bed to put in your room. That wasn't exactly what you had in mind, but your mom isn't going to give you her queen-size bed! Maybe you can push the beds together later.

Friday night you make another deposit — your pay-

check minus $50 cash. **(16D)**

Your car needs gas again. That's $9.57 out of your cash.

On Saturday, your girlfriend arrives with her cousin and a pick-up truck full of furniture and *stuff*. You can't believe it! How in the world will all that fit into your bedroom? You already have the crib in there. Now there's her dresser, desk, and all of her clothes, shoes and boots, tapes and CDs, a box full of make-up and hair stuff, and her school books. Wow! You never knew a girl could have so much stuff. You'd only been in her room once or twice, and you weren't there to look at her furniture.

It takes the whole weekend for you to work out ways to get her settled. You have to clean out part of the garage to store some of your things and the baby stuff that you won't need for awhile.

Your Life Is Changing

The first night, you two talk late into the night about what is happening to your lives. It's scary to realize how much she depends on you now that she isn't living at home. You talk about how much you'd like to have an apartment together, just the two of you — plus the baby, of course.

When you get up the next morning and start to get dressed, half your closet is filled with her clothes, and your bathroom has hair spray and a curling iron in it. It's a weird feeling.

You're still working every afternoon and evening after school. *Deposit your weekly check.* **(17D)**

Your mom tells you that she really needs you to help out with the expenses because it costs a lot to add another person to the household. She's willing to settle for $100 a month for now.

You start to protest, but she reminds you of the extra food to be bought, the extra hot water for showers and laundry, in fact, extra everything that it takes to run a house. You take a deep breath, and agree. She says you need to start now, so *you write her a check for $100.* **(18C)**

That's $100 a month you won't be saving toward a deposit on an apartment. In fact, you're wondering if you'll have money for your next car insurance bill. Your mother has always been very clear on that issue. No liability insurance — no car.

You're beginning to feel trapped. What should you do? Drop out of school and get a job where you can work more hours? And if you make more money, should you get an apartment for you and your girlfriend or should you get a dependable car first so you can get to a better job?

You Decide to Stay in School

You talk to your girlfriend, and after a long conversation, you two realize you'd both better stay in school. Your baby doesn't deserve a dropout parent. You have almost a year of high school left, and your girlfriend has two. Surely you can hang in there for a year with both of you living with your mother. This being somebody's child while you're somebody's parent is weird, but you'll manage.

You and your girlfriend talk about what kind of birth control you'll use once this baby is born. You're sure you don't want to go through this again, and she's sick of being pregnant. She says she *never* wants to get fat like this again.

She makes an appointment at Planned Parenthood, and you go together and learn about all the methods. She agrees to get the Depo-Provera shot every three months after the baby is born. You think that's a good plan.

At the end of the week, you're exhausted from school and working and taking care of your girlfriend, and you haven't seen your buddies at all. Your girlfriend is really tired too. *When you put your $97 into your checking account, you feel a little better.* (**19D**)

Your bank statement came yesterday and you check for errors in your check register. You think the bank has made a mistake because your statement shows nearly $100 less than your check register says. Then you realize one of your deposits wasn't listed yet and *you have a $7.50 service fee to enter in your register.* (**20**) You get it straightened out.

This statement covers Month Two.			
Summary	**Checks/Withdrawals**		**Deposits**
Previous balance 172.90	9C 81.14	14C 12.32	15D 97.00
Deposits 241.00	13C 69.55	18C 100.00	16D 47.00
Withdrawals 263.01			17D 97.00
Service charge 7.50			
New Balance 143.39			

Another week goes by. *You deposit your check.* (**21D**) You need to buy your girlfriend two more maternity tops because she's getting bigger and bigger. *Write a check to Sears for $50.39.* (**22C**)

While you're there, she insists on getting some diapers and three little shirts for the baby. *Write another check to Sears for $37.45.* (**23C**)

You need cash from the bank so *you write a check to Cash for $50.* (**24C**)

You and your girlfriend realize you have to have a mattress and sheets for that crib. You go to JC Penney and look at crib mattresses. You decide the cheaper one will be okay — $50. A waterproof mattress cover costs $18, and you figure you have to have at least three sheets. Knit crib sheets are $9 each. *Total your bill, add 7 percent tax, and write the check.* (**25C**)

Deposit your week's check. (**26D**) *Pay your mom another $100 for your share of the house expenses.* (**27C**)

Celebrating Your Eighteenth Birthday

This week you turn 18. Now you can vote, you can sign contracts on your own, and you can pay child support. You look at your buddies who don't have your responsibilities. One is going to junior college after high school. He wants to be a cop.

Another is planning to be an auto mechanic. He already helps you with your car when it gives you problems.

Another friend is just a goof-off. He doesn't know what to do with his life and he isn't very happy. He just drifts. You're glad you aren't like him, but you feel really old sometimes.

You need some fun. *You write another check to Cash for $50.* (**28C**) You and your girlfriend go out to Sizzler for dinner, then to a movie. It's been a long time since you've been out together. You enjoy dinner and talk mostly about the baby.

Your Baby Arrives

During the movie, her contractions start. It's a long night, getting her to the hospital, worrying about the delivery, then finally seeing your baby. You feel instant love . . . and tremendous responsibility.

The day after your child is born, you drive your girlfriend and your child (who is safely tucked in the car seat you bought) home. Your room is filled with diaper boxes and baby clothes on top of everything else.

You hold the baby while she sleeps and watch while your girlfriend breastfeeds. As interesting as that is, you're glad to be sent to the store for a pacifier and baby wipes and see some sky and breathe air that doesn't smell like baby poop. *Write a check to Payless for $25.78* (**29C**) which includes the pacifier, baby wipes, and flowers for your girlfriend.

Your paycheck this week is only $72 because you missed an afternoon of work when you took your girlfriend and the baby home from the hospital. You decide you have to put it all in your checking account. You'll be staying home nights for awhile anyway. *Deposit $72.* (**30D**)

You have to buy more diapers and baby wipes. The bill is $19.72 including tax. *Write a check to K-Mart.* (**31C**)

You have another paycheck to deposit, but you have to take out $20 in cash because your car is out of gas and you promised your girlfriend you'd take her out for a hamburger tonight. She says she's going stir-crazy staying at home all the time. She's eager to get back to school but that won't be for a couple of weeks. *Deposit $77.* (**32D**)

Your bank statement arrives. Check it out with your check register. *Be sure to deduct your service charge.* (**33**)

This statement covers Month Three					
Summary		**Checks/Withdrawals**			**Deposits**
Previous balance	143.39	22C 50.39	27C 100.00		19D 97.00
Deposits	440.00	23C 37.45	28C 50.00		21D 97.00
Withdrawals	434.99	24C 50.00	29C 25.78		26D 97.00
Service charge	7.50	25C 101.65	31C 19.72		30D 72.00
New Balance	**140.90**				32D 77.00

The High Cost of Diapers

You feel all your money right now may go toward diapers. Your girlfriend says she may switch to formula because it's so hard to breastfeed and go to school. You shudder at the thought of buying formula, too. It's $1 per can, and babies can drink a can every two days. That's $15 per month, and it gets more expensive as the child gets bigger and drinks more. Soon you'll have to buy baby food which can be as high as 69¢ per jar.

Your girlfriend tells you she may qualify for WIC

(Women, Infant and Children Food Program) from the Department of Public Health. That would provide coupons for formula and some of the baby food. That would help.

The diapers will also get more expensive. You've noticed how the diapers are priced. Newborn size is $6.88 for 44 diapers. By the time the kid weighs 26 pounds, though, that same $6.88 only buys 22 diapers. You get half as many! And kids aren't toilet trained for years!

You sit down and figure. There are 365 days in a year. Multiply that by ten diapers a day — 3650 diapers in a year! If $7 buys only 22, how many $7 packages will you have to buy? *Divide 3650 by 22.* **(34)** *Multiply the number of packages by $7.* **(35)** Did you have any idea you'd be spending so much on baby diapers when you were 18 years old?

Expenses Won't Stop

In the middle of all this diaper buying, you have to remember your car insurance. That has to be paid again next month. You still don't have a stroller for your baby, and your girlfriend reminds you that most of the baby clothes she got at her shower are newborn size. Your baby is almost too big for them already.

You're sure you don't want to have more kids until you're older and have more money. You don't want to live with your mom forever, and you don't want to work at this wage forever, but you're pretty stuck right now.

So you do the best you can, you go to school and to work every day, you save as much money as you can, and you're loving to your girlfriend and gentle with your child. You've helped bring a child into this world, and you're helping to make that child feel loved. You wouldn't ever give up your child.

You might have preferred waiting a couple of years . . .

Having a quilt business means long hours of sewing.

CHAPTER 5

You Are an Entrepreneur

You are 18, the mother of a year-old child. You would like to be an entrepreneur — run your own business.

You finally have your high school diploma, and you need to earn some money. Several friends work in a fast-food place, and you tried working there, but you didn't like it. And you didn't like leaving your child for several hours every evening while you went off to work — even though your grandmother took care of him.

You moved in with your grandma the month before your child was born. She agreed to help you with child care while you finished high school. Then you were to get a job and support yourself and your baby. Your grandma works 1-5 P.M. She took care of your child while you attended school in the mornings. But what will you do if you get a full-time job? You don't qualify for jobs that pay more than minimum wage. How will you ever pay for child care? Besides, you hated that fast-food job, and you're not really enthusiastic about other kinds of jobs your friends have.

Can You Work at Home?

You learned to make crib quilts at school, and your teacher says your quilts are the best-looking quilts she's seen. She asked if you ever thought about making more quilts and selling them.

You're very interested in her comments. That would mean you could stay home with your child while you work.

Your teacher reminds you that, if you expect to support your child anytime soon, you'll probably be working harder than you'd ever work at McDonald's. Making quilts in quantity and selling them means *work.* You figure you could handle it. You've never been afraid of work *if* it was something you chose to do.

After talking to your teacher for a long time, then going to your school's career counselor with more questions about marketing, you know you'd like to try it. You're excited. You've always thought it would be great to have your own business rather than working for someone.

Will Your Grandmother Help?

You pay your grandma $150 each month to help with the food and utilities, but you know it would cost a lot more to live by yourself with your baby. Your child's father contributes $100 each month, but that barely covers diapers and baby food. In fact, you don't even put it in your checking account. You only spend it for things your child needs.

A quilt business might be a way to make enough money to be able to stay home with your child.

You share your dream with your grandmother. The problem is, you'd have to have some money to start. You'd probably also have to have help with your child because you know you couldn't sew all day and give your child the attention he needs at the same time.

Your grandma is interested. She says she likes your ambition, and she'd like to help you get started. She says she can take care of your child for three or four hours every morning. You figure you could sew *hard* during those hours and for another couple of hours after your child goes to bed. And you'd be able to do some work while your child is playing. You figure you'd probably be working harder than you ever did at your fast-food job, but this would be *yours.* You think you could do it.

You're thrilled when your grandma gives you $100 to help start your business. *You already have $235 in your checking account,* money you managed to save from your fast-food job. *Add the $100 to your account.* **(1D)**

Getting Your Sales Tax Number

If you sell your quilts to individuals, you have to charge sales tax. Your teacher said that's probably the best place to begin because it's hard to find stores willing to buy items from individuals just starting out. You also need your resale tax number so you can buy supplies for your quilts. With that number, you won't have to pay sales tax on those materials.

Your sales tax number also allows you to buy materials wholesale. You understand wholesalers usually require a minimum purchase of at least $100, but if your quilts sell, you know you'll need to buy large amounts of fabric.

You and your child get on the bus and go down to the nearest State Franchise Tax Board office. You fill out a lot of forms, and you get your resale tax number. You learn

that you'll have to report your total sales every three
months and pay sales tax on everything you sell to
individuals during that time. If you sell your quilts to a
store and they resell to their customers, you are not
responsible for the sales tax.

You're pretty good at math, and you figure you can do it.
Your teacher also said you were welcome to come back and
see her if you need any help.

You also learn that you could have done all this resale
tax number business by phone, assuming you had started
the process two weeks before you sold anything.

Getting Started

Now you're ready to buy some supplies and start making
those crib quilts. You know you have to start small because
your money is limited. You realize that $100 isn't going to
go very far, even when you add it to the $235 you had
already saved.

Your first check is to House of Fabrics for material,
batting, needles, and thread. The total amount for these
items is $34.21.*Write the check.* (**2C**)

In order to make your quilts, you need to have your
sewing machine repaired. That will cost you $35. *Make out
that check to Sew and Vac.* (**3C**) In addition, you need some
more fabric. *Write another check the same day to Normar
Fabrics for $17.93.* (**4C**)

Your First Sale

You sew and sew for four days and produce three quilts.
They are beautiful, and you sell one to your neighbor
immediately. She pays you $50 for the quilt plus 7 percent
sales tax. *Deposit the money.* (**5D**)

You know you have to keep track of the sales tax you
receive because you'll be paying that money to the state at

Sales Record					
Date	Place Sold	# Sold	Price	Sales Tax	Total Price
7/3	Neighbor	1	$50.00	$3.50	$53.50
7/8	Park	2	95.00	6.65	101.65

You keep a record of the quilts you sell.

the end of three months. If you don't have the money when the tax is due, you'll have to pay penalties *and* interest on it. So you decide to write down all your sales in a notebook.

You make six columns, one each for the date, place sold, number sold, quilt price, sales tax, and total price. You vow not to spend that sales tax money until you're ready to send it to the Franchise Tax Board.

You worked *very* hard to make those three quilts. You figure each one takes at least five hours of *uninterrupted* sewing. That means your child is either with your grandma or is asleep. You figure sewing at least six hours each day is a reasonable goal.

Your teacher suggested that $45 to $50 is a fair price, and that if you make a fancier quilt, you might be able to sell it for $55. You look at the cost of your materials, about $15 per quilt. Then you figure how much you're earning per hour. *If they sell,* you'll be making a little more than minimum wage, *and* you'll be home with your child. That sounds better to you than flipping hamburgers.

You remind yourself that you'll also be spending time buying materials and, most important, marketing your quilts. You also didn't allow for the cost of your equipment.

This is *not* going to be easy, but you're determined to make it work.

You take your quilts to the park on Sunday and display them. You're lucky — two of your grandma's friends stop and buy them, one for $45 and another for $50, plus sales tax. *You deposit that money into your account.* **(6D)** *Update your sales record.*

You know you have to get busy and make more quilts and find places to sell them. You love the fabric you've seen at Hancock's, so you take your child and go there and hit a sale. You take along a toy your child hasn't played with for a while so he won't be bored while you shop.

Lucky you, you get $150 worth of fabric, thread, lace, and batting on sale for only $80. *Write them a check.* **(7C)** With this much fabric you figure you can make ten quilts. You go home and get right to it while your child takes his nap. You sew again after he goes to bed for the night.

You work very hard, and five days later, you've made five quilts.

Your child thinks you're *always* sewing. You resolve to take time to play with him, and today you go to the park. He loves going down the slide. You tell yourself you'll stay up two extra hours tonight to catch up on your sewing.

You decide to take your quilts to the Farmer's Market on Tuesday morning. Once there, you are told that you need to have a business license. That costs you $25. *Make the check out to The City of Napa.* **(8C)** Make a note at the bottom of the check and in your check register to remind you of the reason for the check.

People love your quilts, and you sell four that very day for $50 each (plus sales tax). *Deposit the money in your checking account* **(9D)**, *and update your sales record.* You're pretty excited about your sales. You go home and start sewing again.

You Need Better Equipment

For some reason, your sewing machine is giving you trouble. You take it in and the repair person tells you it needs a new motor. A motor costs almost as much as a new machine. You've had your eye on a brand new machine that costs $600.

The sales person will make you a deal and take your old machine in on trade. They will give you $100 for your old machine, and they ask half down on the balance due on the new machine. The rest will be due in one month. You have to include 7 percent sales tax because, unlike the fabric you buy, your machine is for *your* use, and not for resale. *How much will the new machine cost, including tax?* (**10**) *Write out a check for the first payment to Napa Valley Sewing Machines (half the balance on the machine).* (**11C**)

Get busy because you must sell more quilts to pay for that new machine. Remember you have a payment of $250 plus tax due in one month. Using the fabric from your last trip to Hancock's, you manage to make three more quilts.

You are running low on a few items so you and your child go into House of Fabrics and they are having a sale. You spend $85.94 for lace, pins, fabric, batting, and yarn. *Write the check.* (**12C**)

You come home and start sewing. By the end of the week you've made three more quilts.

Marketing Success

The next weekend, you go to the fair in Sonoma and sell six quilts for $50 each plus the sales tax. *Add that up and deposit it into your account.* (**13D**) You take your child with you, and you manage better than you expected. It's hard trying to sell quilts and keep track of a one-year-old at the same time. You decide to ask your grandma to care for your child next time you're out selling quilts.

That made a big difference in your checking account! You are delighted with your new machine and your business. *You happily update your sales chart.*

You make five more quilts in the next week and take them to the Arts and Crafts Fair in Benicia. *You pay a $50 fee for your selling space,* (**14C**), and you sell four quilts. You receive one check for $53.50, another for $48.15, and two checks for $58.85 each, all including sales tax. *Deposit them in your checking account.* (**15D**) *Enter the tax ($14.35) separately in your sales record.* You realize that if you're going to pay a fee to sell your quilts, you'll have to sell more of them to make a profit.

It's the end of the month, so *you write a check to your grandma for $150 for your household expenses.* (**16C**)

Reconciling Your Bank Statement

Your monthly bank statement arrives, and you spend the evening reconciling your checkbook. You know how important it is to know exactly how much money you have in your account.

This statement covers Month One.		Checks/Withdrawals				Deposits	
Summary							
Previous balance	235.00	2C	34.21	8C	25.00	1D	100.00
Deposits	790.15	3C	35.00	11C	267.50	5D	53.50
Withdrawals	595.58	4C	17.93	12C	85.94	6D	101.65
Service charge	13.72	7C	80.00	14C	50.00	9D	214.00
New Balance	**415.85**					13D	321.00

You see that your monthly service charge was $13.72. *Deduct that from your account.* (**17**)

Your checking account balance and the bank's balance match after you figure out the outstanding checks and the last deposit that wasn't yet recorded by the bank.

Reserving the Sales Tax

You add all your deposits from your quilt sales and are thrilled at how much money you've earned. You share your excitement with your grandma, and she asks what you're doing about the sales tax you've collected. You'll have to pay that to the state at the end of the three-month period.

You look at your sales record together. You decide you need to be real clear to yourself about your *spendable* bank balance which does *not* include the sales tax money. You have an idea. At the end of each month you'll add up the sales tax you've received that month. Then you'll deduct that amount from your checking account.

To do this, don't write a check. *Simply itemize "Sales Tax" in your check register, and subtract the amount from your account balance.* (**18ST**) You're amazed at how much sales tax you've already collected.

Getting Ready for the Arts and Crafts Fair

You hear about another arts and crafts fair that will be happening next month. You go back to Hancock's and spend $245 for fabric, batting, new scissors, a rotary cutter and cutting mat — all on sale. *Write the check.* (**19C**)

With the rotary cutter and pad, you save a lot of time in cutting your fabric. You place several layers of cloth on the pad and use the cutter to cut through all the layers at once.

Out of that purchase, you are able to make ten more quilts. In some, you use fabric left over from quilts you made earlier.

You hear that two families on your block have new babies, so you take your quilts over to show them. To your delight, each buys one of your beautiful quilts at $55 each plus sales tax. *Deposit your money.* (**20D**)

You need quilting books for more ideas so you buy some from Normar Fabrics; they cost $23.78. *Write the check.*

(**21C**) Now with lots of new patterns, you make seven more quilts during the next ten days. You're working far harder than you've ever worked in your life, and you're really proud of what you're doing.

You decide you want to back your quilts with flannel since winter is coming. You buy 20 yards of flannel at $4 per yard. *Write that check out to House of Fabrics.* (**22C**)

The Marketing Continues

You know you'll have to beef up your marketing efforts. You can't sell quilts to friends forever! You talk to a friend who thinks she can sell some quilts in Berkeley. She says she'll try if you'll pay her 20 percent commission on whatever she sells. You agree. That seems like a lot of money to "give" to someone else, but you know you have to sell a lot more quilts if your business is to continue.

You also realize you need to know more about record-keeping if you are to succeed at your business. In addition to sales tax, you'll have to know about income tax, and if you ever hire anyone to help you, about employee taxes.

You decide to take a class in adult school this fall. It's a class for small business owners, and you realize that's exactly what you are. There's so much to learn, so much to do.

Sewing seven or eight hours each day sometimes gets old, but then you think of those hamburgers you don't have to cook, and you go back to your sewing machine.

This week you beat your record. You make seven quilts by Saturday. Good for you!

That last payment on your new sewing machine is coming up. *Do you have the amount?* (**23**)

You take your quilts to Farmer's Market again. Good idea! You sell one for $45, one for $55, and three for $50 each, plus sales tax. *Deposit the money.* (**24D**) *Now you can make the final payment to Napa Valley Sewing Machines* *for $267.50.* (**25C**) What a relief!

Your friend, Sue Brown, took twelve of your quilts to the Berkeley crafts fair, and sold ten of them. The checks and cash she gives you total $502.90. *Deposit all the money in your account.* (**26D**) That includes sales tax, so you subtract that amount, $32.90, and pay Sue 20 percent commission on the remaining amount. *Pay her with a check.* (**27C**)

Wow! Look at that money in your account! All it took was determination, lots of time, and a dream. Maybe you can even start putting a little money in a savings account. Maybe you can even save enough to get your own apartment. *You start sewing again.*

Entertaining Your Friends

Since you've been so busy and successful, you haven't seen much of your friends. Invite them over, have pizza delivered, and talk about quilts! *Write a check to Domino's Pizza for $36.50.* (**28C**) You have a great party.

With all that money, you're thinking about what you can do next. Now you decide you can put $200 in a savings account with the Napa Schools Federal Credit Union. *Write a check to the Credit Union.* (**29C**)

With the money you still have in your checking account, you decide to buy your child a toy chest. *Make out the next check to Sears in the amount of $56.78.* (**30C**)

You need a bigger cutting table for your quilt making. You find just the thing at the Thrift Shop, plus you find an old bookcase that you can use to keep your fabric sorted into piles. *Write a check for the total amount: $52.50 including sales tax.* (**31C**)

You take nine quilts to an outdoor craft fair. *You pay a $50 fee to Craft Fair* (**32C**), but it rains and you sell *no* quilts. You can't win them all. There are disappointments in running a business, in addition to lots of satisfaction.

Promoting Your Quilts

You decide that you will advertise your quilting business, so you have 500 cards printed at Action Printing. *Write a check for $24.95.* (**33C**) Your idea is to pin a card to each quilt you sell so people will be able to find you again and request a special quilt. You also know that when you start selling your quilts in stores, you'll need a business card.

You want a good supply of quilts on hand, so you work steadily for a week and produce eight quilts. When you sell them, they have cards attached. Six of the eight quilts sell for $50 each, and the other two, $55 each plus tax. *Add that to your account.* (**34D**) *Update your sales record.*

You have to buy more fabric, so you go to Hancock's Fabrics and buy another pile of flannel, quilting fabric, sewing machine needles, and thread. The total comes to $206.94. *Write the check.* (**35C**)

You are thinking about making some more quilts, so off you go to New York Fabrics in American Canyon, and you find all kinds of new prints. You buy five yards of fabric at $4.69 per yard; eight yards of a special flannel at $4.50 per yard; nine yards of cotton at $3.99 per yard. *Write a check for the total.* (**36C**)

You Get a Special Order

You get started working on quilts but someone calls and wants you to make some on a special order. She needs four quilts in two weeks. The four quilts for that special order sell for $40 each plus tax. *Add that to your account.* (**37D**)

You decide to sign up for another craft fair that has a $55 fee. *Write a check to Mrs. Craft.* (**38C**)

You run out of lace and batting. Go to Hancock's to buy 16 yards of lace at two yards for $1.00, and a huge roll of batting of 20 yards at $2.50 per yard. *Write a check.* (**39C**)

You manage to sell eight of your remaining quilts. You price the eight quilts this way: three at $45 each; one at $50; and four for $55 each. *Add the money for the eight quilts, including tax, to your checking account.* (**40D**) *Be sure you update your sales record.*

The Utilities Cost More

Your grandma gets her electric and gas bill, and finds it's about $45 higher than usual. You talk about it, and figure it's because of all the electricity you're using as you sew. You agree to pay the extra amount. You've also used the phone for taking orders, and that cost, too, has gone up. Your additional share is $15.

Write a check to your grandmother to include the extra utilities, extra phone charge, and her monthly $150. (**41C**)

Another month is gone, and your bank statement arrives.

This statement covers Month Two.						
Summary		**Checks/Withdrawals**				**Deposits**
Previous balance 415.85		16C	150.00	29C	200.00	15D 219.35
Deposits	1717.35	19C	245.00	31C	52.50	20D 117.70
Withdrawals	1584.53	21C	23.78	32C	50.00	24D 267.50
Service charge	14.75	22C	80.00	33C	24.95	26D 502.90
New Balance	533.92	25C	267.50	35C	206.94	34D 438.70
		27C	94.00	36C	95.36	37D 171.20
		28C	36.50	39C	58.00	

You get right to work reconciling the bank balance with your check register. You see that your bank account charge this month was $14.75. *Deduct that from your account balance.* (**42**) You decide to switch your account to the Napa Valley Credit Union to avoid the service charge.

Remember to include the amount you deducted last month for sales tax (**18ST**) when you add up your outstanding checks and other transactions.

Total the sales tax for the past month on your sales record. *Deduct this amount from your checking account balance.* (**43ST**) You'll have to have that money for the State Franchise Tax Board in one more month.

You want to thank your grandmother for giving you the extra money to help you start your business. Your next check is for dinner for two at Chanterelle. That costs $46.45. *Write the check.* (**44C**)

You're a Success!

Your checking account balance looks *good.* You decide to deposit another $200 in your savings account. Write the check. (**45C**) How much money is in your savings account? (**46**) At this rate, you may have money in a few more months for the deposit, first month's rent, and other fees for that apartment you want for you and your child. Exciting!

You've made 55 quilts in two months, and you still have one left to sell. You talk to a friend who owns a store called Things for Kids. She agrees to help you sell your quilts. She says that she will show them in her store, but she takes 40 percent commission on whatever she sells. That seems high, but you agree because this may mean a fairly steady market for your quilts. You hope so.

You have only one quilt left, and it is on display at Things for Kids. To keep your business running, you need to stock up!!! Nobody ever said that supporting yourself was easy, but you've proved it's possible. Now it's back to the sewing machine . . .

Hopefully, this activity has shown you that you really can support yourself using your own talents and skills. Instead of a quilt business, you may choose car detailing, house cleaning, gardening, catering, or . . . Whatever you choose, get going and get on with your life!

Check Form

Reproduce pages 105-108 as Needed

Bank of Any Town, USA

Check No. _____

VOID

Pay to the
Order of _____ $ _____

_____ *Dollars*

Any Student
008/761-0003
000 San Haroldo Way
Anytown, US 06301

Memo _____

20 _____

●●●●✓✗▲✗◇✗❋■❋

Deposit Ticket

Reproduce as Needed

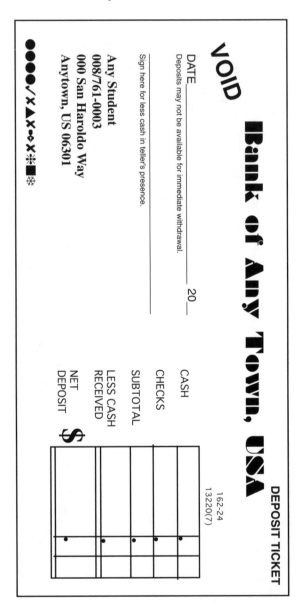

Check Register

Date	Check No.	Transaction	✓	Amount of check	Deposit Amount	Balance

This Worksheet Is Provided
To Help You Balance Your Account

1. Go through your check register and mark off each check, withdrawal, deposit, and other credits listed on your statement. Be sure your register shows any service charges or automatic payments withdrawn from your account during this statement period.
2. Using the chart below, list any outstanding checks and any other withdrawals (including any from previous months) which are listed in your register but are not shown on this statement.
3. Balance your account by filling in the spaces below.

ITEMS OUTSTANDING		
CHECK OR TRANSACTION NO.	AMOUNT	

ENTER
The NEW BALANCE shown on your bank statement $_____

ADD
Any deposits listed in your register $_____
or transfers into your account which $_____
are not shown on your bank statement.   +$_____

TOTAL . . . . + $_____

Calculate the Subtotal. . . . . $_____

SUBTRACT
The total outstanding checks and withdrawals
from the chart above . . . . - $_____

CALCULATE THE ENDING BALANCE
This amount should be the same as the current
balance shown in your check register . . . . $_____

ANNOTATED BIBLIOGRAPHY

The following bibliography contains books of interest to pregnant and parenting teens. Workbooks and other classroom aids are available for some of these titles.

Anasar, Eleanor. **"You and Your Baby: Playing and Learning Together." "You and Your Baby: A Special Relationship."** 2001. **"You and Your Baby: The Toddler Years."** 2003. 32 pp. each. Each available in Spanish edition. $2.65 each. Bulk discounts. The Corner Health Center, 47 North Huron Street, Ypsilanti, MI 48197. 734.484.3600.
Gorgeous photos of teen parents and their children on every other page. Each booklet contains helpful information at extremely easy reading level.

Jacobs, Thomas A., et al. **What Are My Rights? 95 Questions and Answers about Teens and the Law.** 1997. 208 pp. $14.95. Free Spirit Publishing. 612.338.2068.
A matter-of-fact guide to the laws that affect teens at home, at school, on the job, and in their communities.

Lindsay, Jeanne Warren. **The Challenge of Toddlers** and **Your Baby's First Year (Teens Parenting Series).** 2004. 224 pp. each. Paper, $12.95 each; hardcover, $18.95 each. Workbooks, $2.50 each. Quantity discounts. **Challenge of Toddlers** and **Nurturing Your Newborn/Your Baby's First Year Comprehensive Curriculum Notebooks,** $125 each. Morning Glory Press. 888.612.8254.
How-to-parent books especially for teenage parents. Lots of quotes from

teenage parents who share their experiences. Board games ($29.95 each), one for each of these titles, provide great learning reinforcement. Also see four-video series, **Your Baby's First Year,** *($195).*

_____. **Do I Have a Daddy? A Story About a Single-Parent Child.** 2000. 48 pp. Paper, $7.95; hardcover, $14.95. Free study guide. Morning Glory Press.
A beautiful full-color picture book for the child who has never met his/her father. A special sixteen-page section offers suggestions to single mothers.

_____. **Teen Dads: Rights, Responsibilities and Joys (Teens Parenting Series).** 2001. 224 pp. $12.95. Workbook, $2.50. Quantity discounts. **Teen Dads Comprehensive Curriculum Notebook,** $125. (**Notebook** includes one book and one workbook.) Morning Glory.
A how-to-parent book especially for teenage fathers. Offers help in parenting from conception to age 3 of the child. Many quotes from teen fathers.

_____. **Teenage Couples — Caring, Commitment and Change: How to Build a Relationship that Lasts. Teenage Couples — Coping with Reality: Dealing with Money, In-laws, Babies and Other Details of Daily Life.** 1995. 208, 192 pp. Paper, $9.95 ea.; hardcover, $15.95 ea. Workbooks, $2.50 ea. Curriculum Guide, $19.95. Morning Glory Press.
Series covers such important topics as communication, handling arguments, keeping romance alive, sex in a relationship, jealousy, alcohol and drug addiction, partner abuse, and divorce, as well as the practical details of living. Lots of quotes from teenage couples.

_____ and Jean Brunelli. **Nurturing Your Newborn: Young Parent's Guide to Baby's First Month. (Teens Parenting Series)** 1999. 96 pp. $6.95. Workbook, $2. Quantity discounts. Morning Glory Press.
Focuses on the postpartum period. Ideal for teen parents home after delivery. For detailed teaching help, see **Nurturing Your Newborn/Your Baby's First Year Comprehensive Curriculum Notebook.**

_____, _____ . **Your Pregnancy and Newborn Journey (Teens Parenting Series).** 2004. 224 pp. Paper, $12.95; hardcover, $18.95; Workbook, $2.50. **Your Pregnancy and Newborn Journey Comprehensive Curriculum Notebook,** $125. Morning Glory.
Prenatal health book for pregnant teens. Includes section on care of newborn and chapter for fathers. Also see **Pregnancy and Newborn Journey board game** ($29.95) and **Pregnancy Two-in-One Bingo game** ($19.95).

_____ and Sally McCullough. **Discipline from Birth to Three.** 2004. 224 pp. Paper, $12.95; hardcover, $18.95. Workbook, $2.50. **Discipline from Birth to Three Comprehensive Curriculum Notebook,** $125. Morning Glory Press.

Provides teenage parents with guidelines to help prevent discipline problems with children and for dealing with problems when they occur. Also see four-video series, **Discipline from Birth to Three.**

Marecek, Mary. ***Breaking Free from Partner Abuse.*** 1999. 96 pp. $8.95. Quantity discount. Morning Glory Press.
Lovely edition illustrated by Jami Moffett. Underlying message is that the reader does not deserve to be hit. Simply written. Can help a young woman escape an abusive relationship.

_____. ***Moving On: Finding Information You Need for Living on Your Own.*** 2001. 48 pp. $4.95. 25/$75. Morning Glory Press.
Fill-in guide to help young persons find information about their community, information needed for living away from parents.

Porter, Connie. ***Imani All Mine.*** 1999. 218 pp. $12. Houghton Mifflin.
Wonderful novel about a black teen mom in the ghetto where poverty, racism, and danger are constant realities.

Reynolds, Marilyn. **True-to-Life Series from Hamilton High.** *Baby Help. Beyond Dreams. But What About Me? Detour for Emmy. Telling. Too Soon for Jeff. Love Rules. If You Loved Me.* 1993-2001. 160-256 pp. $8.95 each (*Love Rules,* $9.95). Teaching Guides are available. Morning Glory Press.
Wonderfully gripping stories about situations faced by teens. Start with **Detour for Emmy,** *award-winning novel about a 15-year-old mother. Students who read one of Reynolds' novels usually ask for more. Topics cover partner abuse, acquaintance rape, reluctant teen father, sexual molestation, racism, fatal accident, abstinence, homophobia, school failure.*

Seward, Angela. Illustrated by Donna Ferreiro. ***Goodnight, Daddy.*** 2001. 48 pp. Paper, $7.95; hardcover, $14.95. Morning Glory Press.
Beautiful full-color picture book shows Phoebe's excitement because of her father's visit today. She is devastated when he calls to say, "Something has come up." Book illustrates the importance of father in the life of his child.

Williams, Kelly. ***Single Mamahood: Advice and Wisdom for the African American Single Mother.*** 1998. 190 pp. $12. Carol Publishing Group, 120 Enterprise Avenue, Secaucus, NJ 07094.
Down-to-earth, sister-to-sister guide. Offers suggestions on how to deal with work, school, child support, discipline, dating again, and more.

For a current catalog of Morning Glory Press publications:
Telephone 714.828.1998 or 1.888.612.8254   Fax 714.828.2049
e-mail info@morningglorypress.com
Visit web site: www.morningglorypress.com

ABOUT
THE AUTHOR

Sudie Pollock graduated from Napa High School in California in 1964 and returned to the same school district in 1972 as the teacher for the newly funded Pregnant Minor Program which she has headed ever since. She renamed the program *Hill & Valley Teen Parent Program* in recognition of the ups and downs of life.

Over the years, Sudie has also been the district's health education mentor teacher, developing presentations on such topics as "Birth Control Is Life Control," "Sexually Transmitted Diseases in Pictures," "Labor and Delivery," and "How Parenthood Changes Your Life."

She has been a volunteer trainer for Planned Parenthood, a volunteer with the local Child Abuse Prevention Hot Line, and is a licensed Marriage, Family, and Child therapist. In 2000 she was acclaimed a community hero by the Napa County Board of Supervisors. Her feminist beliefs spill over into her teaching, empowering her young parents with new strength.